Richer Entanglements

Poets on Poetry   **Donald Hall, General Editor**

DONALD HALL	*Goatfoot Milktongue Twinbird*
GALWAY KINNELL	*Walking Down the Stairs*
WILLIAM STAFFORD	*Writing the Australian Crawl*
DONALD DAVIE	*Trying to Explain*
MAXINE KUMIN	*To Make a Prairie*
DIANE WAKOSKI	*Toward a New Poetry*
ROBERT BLY	*Talking All Morning*
RICHARD KOSTELANETZ	*The Old Poetries and the New*
LOUIS SIMPSON	*A Company of Poets*
PHILIP LEVINE	*Don't Ask*
JOHN HAINES	*Living Off the Country*
MARGE PIERCY	*Parti-Colored Blocks for a Quilt*
DONALD HALL	*The Weather for Poetry*
JAMES WRIGHT	*Collected Prose*
ALICIA OSTRIKER	*Writing Like a Woman*
JOHN LOGAN	*A Ballet for the Ear*
HAYDEN CARRUTH	*Effluences from the Sacred Caves*
ROBERT HAYDEN	*Collected Prose*
JOHN FREDERICK NIMS	*A Local Habitation*
ANNE SEXTON	*No Evil Star*
CHARLES SIMIC	*The Uncertain Certainty*
LOUIS SIMPSON	*The Character of the Poet*
WILLIAM STAFFORD	*You Must Revise Your Life*
TESS GALLAGHER	*A Concert of Tenses*
WELDON KEES	*Reviews and Essays, 1936–55*
DONALD HALL	*Poetry and Ambition*
CHARLES WRIGHT	*Halflife*
WILLIAM MATTHEWS	*Curiosities*
CHARLES SIMIC	*Wonderful Words, Silent Truth*
TOM CLARK	*The Poetry Beat*
WILLIAM MEREDITH	*Poems Are Hard to Read*
PETER DAVISON	*One of the Dangerous Trades*
AMY CLAMPITT	*Predecessors, Et Cetera*
JANE MILLER	*Working Time*
DAVID LEHMAN	*The Line Forms Here*
HAYDEN CARRUTH	*Suicides and Jazzers*
DANIEL HOFFMAN	*Words to Create a World*
GREGORY ORR	*Richer Entanglements*

Gregory Orr

Richer

Entanglements

ESSAYS AND NOTES ON POETRY AND POEMS

Ann Arbor

THE UNIVERSITY OF MICHIGAN PRESS

Copyright © by the University of Michigan 1993
All rights reserved
Published in the United States of America by
The University of Michigan Press
Manufactured in the United States of America

1996 1995 1994 1993   4 3 2 1

Library of Congress Cataloging-in-Publication Data
Orr, Gregory.
   Richer entanglements : essays and notes on poetry and poems / Gregory Orr.
      p.   cm.—(Poets on poetry)
   Includes bibliographical references (p.).
   ISBN 0-472-09525-0 (alk. paper). — ISBN 0-472-06525-4 (pbk. : alk. paper)
   1. Orr, Gregory—Aesthetics. 2. Poetics. 3. Poetry. I. Title.
PS3565.R7R5   1993
809.1—dc20   93-10796
                                                                CIP

A CIP catalogue record for this book is available from the British Library.

*Richer entanglements, enthralments far
More self-destroying . . .*
—Keats, *Endymion*

Acknowledgments

Grateful acknowledgment is made to the following journals and publishers for permission to reprint previously published material:

American Poetry Review for "The Poems of Stanley Kunitz," *APR*, 1979; for "Four Temperaments and the Forms of Poetry," *APR* 17, no. 5 (Oct./Nov. 1988); for "The Two-Way Ladder: On the Friendship and Mutual Influence between Elizabeth Bishop and Robert Lowell," *APR* 20, no. 5 (Sept./Oct. 1991).

Associated Writing Programs Newsletter for "The Interrupted Scheme: Some Thoughts on Disorder and Order in the Lives of Poets and the Lives of Poems," *AWP Newsletter,* Nov. 1988.

Indiana Review and Fairleigh Dickinson University Press for "Harp of Lost Worlds: A Conversation with Gregory Orr," *Indiana Review* 10, no. 3 (Spring 1987) and *The Post-Confessionals: Conversations with American Poets of the Eighties,* edited by Earl G. Ingersoll, Judith Kitchen, and Stan Sanvel Rubin (Rutherford, N.J.: Fairleigh Dickinson University Press, 1989).

Iowa Review and Story Line Press for "A Reading of Donald Hall's 'Kicking the Leaves,'" *Iowa Review* 18, no. 1 (Winter 1988), and *The Day I Was Older: On the Poetry of Donald Hall,* edited by Liam Rector (Santa Cruz: Story Line Press, 1989).

Ontario Review Press for "Some Notes" from *The Generation of 2000,* edited by William Heyen (Princeton: Ontario Review Press, 1984).

Poetry East and Beacon Press for "The Need for Poetics: Thoughts on Robert Bly," *Poetry East* 4/5 (Spring/Summer 1981) and *Of Solitude and Silence: Writings on Robert Bly,* edited by Richard Jones and Kate Daniels (Boston: Beacon Press, 1981).

Seneca Review for "Notebook Excerpts," *Seneca Review* 21, no. 2 (Winter 1992).

Willow Review for "Remarks on Craft," *Willow Review* 19 (Spring 1992).

Every effort has been made to trace the ownership of copyrighted material in this book and to obtain permission for its use.

Contents

I. Order and Disorder

Four Temperaments and the Forms of Poetry	3
The Interrupted Scheme: Some Thoughts on Disorder and Order in the Lives of Poets and the Lives of Poems	15
Order and Disorder in Lyric Poetry	24
Two Anecdotes about Masks	36

II. Lyric to Dramatic Lyric

Keats and Yeats: From Lyric to Dramatic Lyric	41
A Cluster of Quotations and Notes	66

III. Some Poets

A Reading of Donald Hall's "Kicking the Leaves"	87
The Poems of Stanley Kunitz	97
The Need for Poetics: Some Thoughts on Robert Bly	126
The Two-Way Ladder: Bishop and Lowell	132

IV. Conversations, Comments, and Notes

Conversation at Brockport	151
Some Notes	163

Some Remarks on Craft	165
Notebook Excerpts	168
From a Commonplace Book	174

I

Order and Disorder

Four Temperaments and the Forms of Poetry

Now there are diversities of gifts but the same Spirit.
—1 Corinthians 12:4

I'd like to propose that poets are born with a certain innate form-giving temperament that allows them to forge language into the convincing unities we call poems. This form-giving gift is more important than any other a poet might possess. Different poets are born with different temperaments, and the nature of their temperaments determines essential qualities of the poems they write.

To my way of thinking, there are four distinct temperaments. If a poet is born with one temperament, then he or she grows as a poet by developing that temperament, but *also* by nurturing the others. The greatest poem is one in which all four temperaments are present in the strongest degree, though no one in English but Shakespeare could be said to exhibit all four in equal vigor. The main point is, great poems show the presence of all four, though in varying proportions.

A Glance at Characteristics and Dynamics

The four temperaments are: story, structure, music, and imagination.

1. Story: dramatic unity—beginning, middle, and end. Conflict, dramatic focus, resolution.

American Poetry Review (1988).

2. Structure: the satisfaction of measurable patterns. It is akin to higher math, geometry, theoretical physics—the beauty and balance of equations. It manifests itself in sonnets, villanelles, sestinas (closed structures) and, to a lesser extent, in metrical lines, rhymed couplets, and repeated stanza patterns (open structures).
3. Music: rhythm and sounds. It includes syntax, the syllabic qualities of English that determine rhythm (pitch, duration, stress, loudness/softness), and the entire panoply of sound effects (alliteration, assonance, consonance, internal rhyme, etc.). (I realize that music is an old metaphor for the texture of rhythm and sounds in a poem, and perhaps not a very adequate one, but I'm going to use it anyway.)
4. Imagination: the flow of image to image or thought to thought. It moves as a stream of association, either concretely (the flow of image) or abstractly (the flow of thought).

It is essential to recognize that the four temperaments form another pattern. Story and structure are *intensive* in their impulse; music and imagination are *extensive*. Story and structure concern limits and correspond to our desire for and recognition of the role of law. Music and imagination concern our longing for liberty, the unconditional and limitless.

Limiting impulse:	Limitlessness:
Story	Music
Structure	Imagination

Although each of the temperaments is capable, in and of itself, of creating the unity we call a poem, for a poem to have the stability and dynamic tension that comes of a marriage of contraries it must fuse a limiting impulse with an impulse that resists limitation. Thus Dylan Thomas's most successful poems are those in which his primary musical temperament is constrained by the limiting qualities of structure (the villanelle "Do Not Go Gentle into That Good Night") or of story (the minor but effective story progressions of "Poem in October" or "Over

Sir John's Hill"). Likewise, Richard Wilbur's structural temperament has need of those qualities that resist limitation, as when the run-on syntax, alliteration, and elaborately varied vowels of "A Baroque Wall-Fountain in the Villa Sciarra" enact a watery music that flows around and over the structure.

If the minimum formula for a poem's success is a kind of Chinese menu—one from Column A (the limits of story and structure), one from Column B (the limitlessness of music and imagination)—then it should be added that combining two impulses from the same column can be fatal. Hart Crane's reputation, despite his great gifts, is precarious in large part because he so frequently relied on a fusion of music and imagination to make his poems. One can say the same of Dylan Thomas, or Swinburne for that matter. Such a marriage makes it almost impossible to create closure, to constellate a wholeness. If the dangers of a music/imagination combination are quite obvious, the converse—a fusion of story and structure—also presents characteristic problems. The prime example of this is the later Wordsworth. His great early work was sustained by a tension between the poles of imagination and story. When he lost faith in his basic story of the benign interfusing of man and nature ("Elegaic Stanzas on a Painting of Peele Castle in Storm" dramatizes this loss), Wordsworth felt burdened and alarmed by the chaotic flow of imagination ("Me this unchartered freedom tires" he laments in "Ode to Duty"). His response was to repudiate imagination and turn to structure. Seeking "brief solace" in the rigidity of their structural constraints, he created hundreds of hollow sonnets through which his basic story echoes faintly, unconvincingly.

Story

Aristotle is full of insights into the nature of story: the primary importance of action and event; the need to create dramatic focus around a single action. "So too the plot of the play, being the representation of an action, must present it as a unified whole; and its various incidents must be so arranged that if anyone of them is differently placed or taken away the effect of wholeness will be seriously disrupted" (*Poetics*, chap. 8, Penguin translation).

The role of beginning, middle, and end; that beauty is the result of the harmonious proportion of parts; how the power of "discovery" and "reversal" function as pivot points in the best stories.

Story is magical. When Coleridge's Ancient Mariner intones " 'There was a ship' quoth he . . ." we are at the beginning of story and we, like the Wedding Guest, yield to its enthralling power—"listen[ing] like a three years' child."

Thomas Wyatt's poem establishes the essential conflict of story in the pronouns of its opening line: "They flee from me that sometime did me seek." And his second stanza goes on to reveal the extraordinary focusing power of story: "but once, in special: / in thin array, after a pleasant guise."

Conflict is essential to story—without conflict there is no dramatic tension. As Blake says: "Without Contraries is no Progression." This conflict at the source of story is what the poem resolves, as in the Renaissance motto, "Harmonia est discordia concors" (Harmony is discord reconciled).

Hollywood's oldest formula for story corresponds well to Aristotle's terms if not his spirit: boy meets girl, boy loses girl, boy gets girl. But the conflict that is the essential ingredient of story needn't be something out of melodrama. What is essential to story is that there be at least two centers of energy, two poles of awareness around which the conflict can organize itself. In poetry, the mere presence of two discrete pronouns (such as Wyatt's "They flee from me") is sufficient to create the tension that story will resolve.

When Stanley Kunitz counsels young poets to "polarize their contradictions," he is proposing that one source of dramatic conflict can be ambivalence within the individual. Such a formula is related to Yeats's remark—"out of our quarrels with others we make rhetoric, out of our quarrels with ourselves poetry." It is the self-quarrel of attraction and repulsion vis-à-vis sensuality that galvanizes Eliot's "The Love Song of J. Alfred Prufrock."

But of course, the dramatic conflict is just as likely to concern two figures in the world, as in Robert Hayden's "Those Winter Sundays," where father and son enact their tragic dance of misunderstanding and fear.

Or the self is at odds with the external world; either the social/political world, as in Yeats's "Lapis Lazuli" or "Among School Children," or the natural world, as in his "The Wild Swans at Coole."

Yeats provides further insight into the nature of story when, in a letter written a few weeks before his death, he speaks of trying to put everything he knows into a single sentence and arriving at "Man can embody truth, but he cannot know it." The *embodied* meanings of event, gesture, and deed are how story expresses its truths.

Story is the embodied truth of contraries seeking resolution. Story, in poetry, is seldom concerned with the elaborate and unpredictable contingencies of the world we live in; those belong to fiction. Nor is story in poetry narrative (a larger, looser term). In story, events constellate around a single conflict (Aristotle's "unity of action").

In the twentieth century, the psychological century, Freud has proposed specific archetypal stories such as those underlying the Oedipus complex and the Electra complex. More broadly, he has drawn our attention to the family triad (father, mother, child) as a rich source of urgent stories. Sometimes poets have organized them as a two-person conflict, as in Plath's "Daddy" or Adrienne Rich's "Snapshots of a Daughter-in-Law"; other times they have been dramatized with triadic richness as in Louis Simpson's "My Father in the Night Commanding No," Stanley Kunitz's "The Portrait," and Roethke's "My Father's Waltz."

Structure

The structural temperament expresses itself in pattern making in a profound sense. This temperament can manifest itself in either open or closed structures. By open structures I mean such things as metrical lines or the infinitely extensible form of rhymed couplets. A poem consisting of metrical stanzas is also an open structure. A closed structure would be something like a sonnet, a villanelle, or a sestina, all of whose defining limits can be seen as approaching an ideal.

In order properly to appreciate the structural temperament, we must realize that for poets of this temperament the beauty of pattern is itself a form of meaning. The transcendent aspirations of such a temperament bring to mind this passage from Plato's *Philebus:*

> The beauty of figures which I am now trying to indicate is not what most people would understand as such, not the beauty of a living creature or a picture; what I mean . . . is something straight, or round, and the surfaces and solides which a lathe or a carpenter's rule and square produces from the straight and the round. Things like that . . . are beautiful, not in a relative sense; they are always beautiful in their very nature, and they carry pleasures peculiar to themselves and which are free of the itch of desire.

A statement from a structural perspective: "The correction of prose, because it has no fixed laws, is endless; a poem comes right with a click like a box" (Yeats in a letter to Dorothy Wellesley).

The structural temperament will always place great emphasis on the conscious pattern-making intention of the poet. The epitome of this, almost a parody, is Edgar Allan Poe's essay, "The Philosophy of Composition," in which he elaborately sets forth his construction of "The Raven."

To poets whose gift is for structure, structure is *primary,* an essence. It isn't something imposed on the poem, not even something chosen in the ordinary sense of the word. It certainly is wrong (how much blood has been spilled on this false issue) to contrast structure with free verse, as if it were simply an esthetic choice rather than a fundamental form-giving impulse in certain poets. Ezra Pound, usually so perceptive about poetry, is uncharacteristically dismissive of "symmetrical forms." Intent as he is on promulgating a new sense of rhythm and a new idea of the nature and role of the image, he betrays a significant lack of sympathy for the structural temperament when he warns, "don't put in what you want to say and then fill up the vacuums with slush" (from "Imagisme," *Poetry*, 1913). In fact, Pound also rejects the other limiting impulse, story, having incorporated "the great discovery of the French symbolists," which was "the irrelevance and hence the possibility of abolition of paraphrasable plot" (Kenner, *The Art of Ezra Pound*, p. 9). Given these rejections of the limiting temperaments, it's not surprising that Pound's "three kinds of poetry" (melopoeia, phanopoeia, and logopoeia, from the essay "How to Read") in fact only represent the two limitless temperaments, melopoeia corresponding to music, phanopoeia to concrete imagination, and logopoeia to abstract imagination. Such blindness to the role of the limiting impulses had severe consequences for Pound's own later poetry as it struggled to find a convincing and cohering form.

That the great majority of poems written in English since the sixteenth century have aspired to metrical regularity and used a pattern of rhyme and stanzaic repetition does not mean that they are all products of structural temperaments. One need only consider Donne, whose temperament is clearly centered in imagination, the flow of one image or idea into another. If lasting poetry demands metrical regularity, then Ben Jonson was right and Donne did "for not keeping of accent, deserve hanging." But Coleridge comes closer to Donne's genius of imagination when he declares that its power and purpose is to "wreathe iron pokers into true-love knots."

Music

The musical temperament manifests itself in the individual qualities of syllables (pitch, duration, stress, loudness/softness), in syntax, and in assorted sound effects (assonance, consonance, alliteration, and subtler phenomena) as they interact to create the poem's aural and rhythmical structure.

Music in poetry is irrational; it works directly on the emotions, regardless of the purported content of the language. Primitive and powerful. Dionysus' flute rather than Apollo's lyre—more ecstasy and trance than measure and order. Thus Plato bans from his ordered republic certain musical modes (and the poems associated with them) because they have the power to generate undesirable emotions in their hearers.

The cadences of evangelists, orators, and demagogues—the undeniable, even physiological response, but casting a deeply ambiguous moral light.

Primitive in an emotional sense, but also ontologically primitive in the individual—the infant's joy in the babble and coo of sound, the child's pleasure in nursery rhymes. When Coleridge insists that "the sense of musical delight, with the power of producing it in others" is an essential prerequisite for a poet, he places musical pleasure at the very center of poetry.

No matter how carefully you analyze Hart Crane's "Voyages" in terms of imagistic unity, the fact remains that music makes the poem cohere. There is no question that thematic patterns are developed and fulfilled in Keats's "To Autumn"—but its power and unity derive from the same source as its pleasures: a masterful manipulation of sound and rhythm. We hear it in the elaborate musical/emotional parabolas of Roethke's "The Lost Son."

Music shares with imagination the difficulties of closure. In many completed and fulfilled patterns of sound and rhythm, there is still something left over, some vowel, say, that calls out across the poem's final period to its fellow in the silence beyond, asking to go further, to generate new possibilities and combinations. When Keats, in *Endymion,* deliberately and constantly enjambed his couplets, he created a self-defeating structure, especially since he had no story grip on the poem—and so it flowed ("You will be glad to hear that within these last three weeks I have written 1000 Lines" he writes to Haydon), formless, a sweet meander.

And yet, when a poem of musical temperament resolves successfully, it does so by a powerful marshaling of its inherent qualities, as in the extraordinary last line of Hopkins's "Thou art indeed just, Lord": "Mine, O thou lord of life, send my roots rain." The two heavy internal pauses, the alliteration, the fact that each of the last four monosyllables is heavily stressed, the assonantal thread of the long "i" (mind, life, my) and the extraordinary variety of vowel pitch playing off against this assonance—all these factors impinge on the line with an authority that can only be followed by silence.

Imagination

A poet can, and frequently does, possess both an abstract and a concrete imagination, but sometimes there is a peculiar antipathy among these poets of imagination, for instance, the hostility and condescension Pound and Williams (both finally poets of abstract imagination in my opinion) felt toward Whitman, a poet of decidedly concrete imagination.

A few poets of imagination: Donne, George Herbert (abstract imagination), Blake in his "Prophetic Books," Wordsworth, Whitman (concrete imagination), Dickinson, Rimbaud, Pound, William Carlos Williams, Eliot, George Oppen, Pablo Neruda.

With imagination, as with music, it is easier to recognize its presence as the dominant form-giving temperament in particular poets than it is to characterize the temperament itself. Why is this? Perhaps because an individual poet's imagination moves in ways so peculiar and particular to him or her—so Wordsworth would seem to say in the very poem in which he endeavors to set forth both the principles and processes of his own imagination:

> Not only general habits and desires,
> But each most obvious and particular thought,
> Not in a mystical and idle sense,
> But in the words of reason deeply weigh'd,
> Hath no beginning.
>
> (*The Prelude* 2, lines 232–37)

Even when we can trace an individual poet's way of moving by imagination, it doesn't mean that we can pull back and generalize about the process of imagination itself, in part because it *is* a process and has a way of quicksilvering through our hands—we're like Menelaus trying to capture the metamorphosing Proteus in book 4 of *The Odyssey*.

Having said that, it's worth looking at section 6 of Whitman's "Song of Myself" in order to watch an imaginative temperament unfolding explicably and inexplicably in language. In the opening lines, the poem (and the temperament) frees itself by associative "guesses" from an analytical, descriptive stance toward reality:

> A child said *What is the grass?* fetching it to me with full hands,
> How could I answer the child? I do not know what it is any more than he.
>
> I guess it must be the flag of my disposition, out of hopeful green stuff woven.
>
> (lines 1–3)

And then launches into the dizzying and audacious metaphors that are the poem's lifeblood:

> Or I guess it is the handkerchief of the Lord,
> A scented gift and remembrancer designedly dropt,
> Bearing the owner's name someway in the corners, that we may see and remark, and say *Whose?*
>
> Or I guess the grass is itself a child, the produced babe of the vegetation.
>
> (lines 4–7)

We can analyze Whitman's leaps: that he consolidates the general term "grass" into a rectangular shape with "flag" and this suggests "woven" and the two together result in the image of the handkerchief. But what analysis is adequate to the awesomely condensed implications of the resulting image: God (as a woman?) has flirtatiously dropped the perfumed handkerchief we know as grass so that we, according to the elabo-

12

rate rituals of assignation or courtship, might thus seek out the divine creator? And this is only three lines—no sooner presented than cast aside for a further image, and another one after that.

How than does a poem governed by the imaginative temperament overcome its own centrifugal impulses and finally cohere? Again, the Whitman poem might give us one important answer—even the wildest, most free-ranging imagination has its themes and obsessions, which it tends to circle around. When, in line 12, Whitman introduces this metaphor for grass—"And now it seems to me the beautiful uncut hair of graves"—he has stumbled upon one of his fundamental thematic obsessions, death. For the remaining twenty-one lines of the poem, the imagination circles in an obsessive spiral around images of graves and death. This fierce spiral shape is not the scattering violence of a tornado, but that of a whirlpool sucking into its centripetal vortex the most disparate objects. And there at the still point of the whirlpool's bottom, one passes through (as if it were really the narrow part of an hourglass) and catches a glimpse of the expanding calm beyond—"All goes onward and outward, nothing collapses, / and to die is different from what anyone supposed, and luckier."

Eros and Thanatos are two deep channels in the wide river of imagination, and quite often the two channels join and roil together their currents. It's easier to generalize about a poet of concrete imagination like Whitman, whose poems are frequently in contact with Eros and Thanatos and their lesser attendant mysteries and emotions, than about someone like Pound or Oppen, whose poems of abstract imagination give the impression of being freer from the cohesive or focusing power of these two major human obsessions. Perhaps one could argue that abstract imaginations are characterized by a "train of thought." Literalizing that dead metaphor for a moment, we might say that each thought, idea, or didactic anecdote is a baggage or passenger car—a discrete unit yet linked to its counterparts and propelled by another discrete unit, the engine, which has energy sufficient to give the whole train movement and purpose.

A Few Thoughts for Poets

It's possible to imagine a poet who proceeds entirely by instinct, one poem succeeding another in a dazzle of ignorant bliss. But all real poets also exist in the long spaces between poems, where a lot of thought takes place. A poet is always trying to decide who he or she is and might become. To me, the notion of the four temperaments holds the promise of an underlying pattern that can orient and guide a poet as well as a critic.

The first issue is always one of self-knowledge or self-recognition. Once a poet has a sense of his or her fundamental temperament, the possibilities for growth are twofold. The first is to go further into the gift, but such a decision carries with it the risk of narrowing as well as the promise of deepening.

The second direction is to expand. Such an expansion can be understood as the poet's struggle to nurture and develop the other temperaments in such a way that their energies and constraints enrich his or her poems. Again, no one can hope to have all four temperaments in equal strength, but the goal will always be to have all four temperaments present, though some will arrive as gifts and others must be learned and labored for.

The Interrupted Scheme
Some Thoughts on Disorder and Order in the Lives of Poets and the Lives of Poems

> *[Imagination] reveals itself in the balance or reconciliation of opposite or discordant qualities: . . . a more than usual state of emotion with more than usual order.*
> —Coleridge, *Biographia Literaria*

Coleridge, who was one of the first to introduce the word "psychological" into English, gives us formulations that go to the heart of poetry's human importance. Faced with disorder, the human mind needs to respond with an ordering principle that will sustain it and console it. Nowhere is that more graphically evident than when individual victims of violent crimes like rapes or muggings struggle to cope with the event. Again and again, they construct poignant and pathetic retrospective stories ("If only I hadn't . . .") that *prove* the world is not random disorder. Rather than accept that they were simply in the wrong place at the wrong time, they will "blame themselves," as so many of these stories do, if that is the only way they can assert that some ordering principle does indeed determine what happens in the world.

We all know the overwhelming power of chance, accident, randomness, disorder. How lives, our lives, can be altered or ended abruptly, catastrophically. It's a truth we can't live without and can't live with. It's a truth that calls up a countertruth: the human need to believe in ordering principles, even if we have to invent them ourselves. And that is what the human imagination does—the victim going over the event

---

Associated Writing Programs Newsletter (1988).

again and again is trying to create or discover the ordering principle, the story, that will make it bearable.

And don't poems do the same thing? Don't they present us with a disorder that represents the randomness we feel threatened by in our lives and then respond with an ordering that seems to answer that disorder? Isn't that what makes poems vital—a genuinely threatening sense of disorder and an equally convincing order? The two forces together seek some balance, reconciliation, or resolution.

In poems, disorder tends to be thematic. Love and Death, the great lyric themes, are essentially disordering as they impinge on the individual life. Think of Dickinson's poem "I cannot live with You," where love is so deeply disruptive as to cause her to offend even divine order. Yet not all disorder is destructive. In the West, love's disorder may be pleasurable and vitalizing, as in Herrick's "Delight in Disorder" ("A sweet disorder in the dress / Kindles in clothes a wantonness"), though here the theme of arousing disarray unfolds in the context of the ordering of costume just as his plea for disorder is expressed in the context of highly ordered rhymed couplets.

Disorder can be present formally as well as thematically. French Surrealism utilized an intentional formal disorder of syntax and imagery as a means of social and political revolt in pursuit of that higher ordering promised by the term itself, defined by Breton in the First Manifesto as a resolution of the two states of dream and reality into a higher or sur-reality. The surrealist poem, a late Romantic development, uses a formal disorder in the services of a higher order, just as Rimbaud's "long, intentional disordering of all the senses" was the necessary disorder of the life that led to the creation of the higher order of "voyant," or visionary poet.

Order, the ordering principle, can also be either thematic or formal. In terms of thematic ordering, we may no longer be as convinced of the cosmic governing principles of divine love and harmony as Sir John Davies was when he constructed his hundreds of lines of "Orchestra," in which all nature from insects to galaxies did its formal dance, but we are still easily convinced that love orders our lives. And meter, rhyme, and traditional forms, the primary historical ordering principles of poetry, again and again assert their power. Not to mention the fact that each poem in the tradition becomes a model for subsequent poems and endorses their orderings when it is imitated, evoked, or alluded to.

Poems that continue to engage us enact this contest, this Aristotelean agon of disorder and order. The poem unfolds or initiates its particular version of disorder only to have it answered by a final sense that (to use a phrase from Robert Duncan's poem) "certain bounds hold against chaos."

Individuals vary enormously in their sense of what is genuinely threatening and what is adequately ordering, and much disagreement over the "greatness" of this or that poet or poem really hinges on the subjective response of the reader to these issues. This response, in turn, has been created by the circumstances of the reader's life and his or her innate temperament. In this deep sense "de gustibus non est disputandum" holds—there's no arguing taste. It's like the first time you move in with another person and discover that the way they arrange their furniture and physical space can be nonnegotiable, your two distinct senses of order and disorder creating a series of tensions and collisions curious in their intensity.

I think it's fair to say that poetry exerts a powerful attraction on people who have an intense consciousness of disorder. The art has an enormous reservoir of ordering principles and historical models which it offers the individual as he or she enacts the "difficult balance" of making sense of the world. However, the very ordering powers of poetry can represent a possible danger. What if, in the complex interaction between the poet and the poem, the poem comes to represent *only* an ordering—what if its order suffocates all wildness in the process of offsetting the psychic imbalance of the poet?

Gerard Manley Hopkins is a wonderful example of someone impelled by a need for strong ordering principles, both in his life and in his art. I wish to sketch his ordering efforts, not belabor them, because my goal is to focus some thoughts and perceptions on a particular poem of his.

Perhaps the clearest hint about Hopkins's personality is contained in a letter of 1882 to Robert Bridges. After denying Whitman's influence on his own work, Hopkins says the following:

> But first I may as well say what I should not otherwise have said, that I always knew in my heart Walt Whitman's mind to be more like my own than any other man's living. As he is a great scoundrel this is not a pleasant confession. And this also makes me the more desirous to read him and the more determined that I will not.

How that last sentence reverses itself perfectly in mid-sentence—desire leading not to the acts that fulfill it, but to a moral determination to resist, to turn against that with which he identifies. He slams the door in Whitman's face, Whitman who would have all doors removed from their hinges. Why? Both Whitman and Hopkins were exquisite sensibilities—intense and emotional in their response to nature and to sensation:

> Is this then a touch? quivering me to a new identity,
> Flames and ether making a rush for my veins,
> Treacherous tip of me reaching and crowding to help them,
> My flesh and blood playing out lightning to strike what is
>   hardly different from myself
>
> (Song of Myself, sec. 28)

Where they differed is in their response to this intense sensibility that they possessed, that possessed them. Whitman felt confident that he could give his sensibility celebratory expression and that this expression would discover or create an adequate new form for it, that the "original energy without check" he "permitted to speak" would create or discover an original ordering principle. That he was right in his risk is the glad judgment of history.

But Hopkins had no such confidence, either for his person or for its expression in language. And so he took this wild spirit, this chaotic sensibility he recognized in himself, and submitted it to numerous successive and progressively more stringent orderings to make it either bearable or acceptable. He converted to Catholicism and became a priest (celibacy—a rejection of the disturbing erotic component of his personality), and then past that to joining the Jesuits, the soldiers of Christ, severe, ascetic, disciplined. (Imagine Whitman as a Jesuit!)

As part of his religious renunciations, he gave up poetry entirely, only returning to it seven years later, when, at the request of his rector, he composed "The Wreck of the *Deutschland*"—in part to memorialize the five Franciscan nuns who perished in the shipwreck. The poems he subsequently wrote had to be theologically acceptable, to confirm and conform to his religious compass and that of his order.

Another entire essay could be written about how, "safe" in the double ordering of life and art form, Hopkins felt finally free to let his disorder loose. Nor is that disorder simply the thematic anguish of his so-called "dark sonnets." It manifests itself constantly in rhythms, sounds, and syntax:

> As kingfishers catch fire, dragonflies draw flame;
> As tumbled over rim in roundy wells
> Stones ring; like each tucked string tells each hung bell's
> Bow swung finds tongue to fling out broad its name.

Even his sonnet forms disorder into "curtal sonnets" and other invented variants. This upheaval within the double ordering of life and art is like an orgy taking place inside a locked room inside a locked house. That we still read Hopkins with interest and pleasure attests that he was right to impose such restraints.

But I want to focus here on one small phenomenon of disorder in a poem of profound order and beauty.

> *Spring and Fall*
> to a young child
>
> Margaret, are you grieving
> Over Goldengrove unleaving?
> Leaves, like the things of man, you
> With your fresh thoughts care for, can you?

19

> Ah! as the heart grows older
> It will come to such sights colder
> By and by, nor spare a sigh
> Though worlds of wanwood leafmeal lie;
> And yet you will weep and know why.
> Now no matter, child, the name:
> Sorrow's springs are the same.
> Nor mouth had, no nor mind, expressed
> What heart heard of, ghost guessed:
> It is the blight man was born for,
> It is Margaret you mourn for.

"Spring and Fall" even in its title proposes a balancing of birth and decay. According to the poem's symbolic structure, the theme of disorder written in human terms is mortality, written in vegetative nature's terms is decay; further, that the two are parallel and even interfused in a deeply felt, primal way.

But it is the subtitle that interests me: "to a young child." The subtitle announces another person to whom the poem is presumably addressed. The *reference* to another person is itself unusual in Hopkins's poetry, but this child is not a reference, she is a *presence* in the poem. The poem's opening word is her name, "Margaret," and the same name will return to give the last line its power and poignancy. Alerted to her existence in the poem, we could alter Yeats's title and say: in names begin responsibilities. This girl is not simply a symbol, the "spring" end of the symbolic seesaw, but a dramatic presence in the poem. In the highly ordered world of Christian Hopkins, it is rare to find another person. Typically, nature, God, and the poet's emotions come together to confirm a cosmic order. But such an order has, in Hopkins, a tendency to exclude other humans, to exclude human otherness. It is the disorder of Margaret's human otherness that challenges Hopkins's ordering impulse to deepen and enlarge its embrace.

The poem's opening lines present a dramatic situation: the speaker and the girl are confronting each other. The girl is upset (perhaps they are in the woods called Goldengrove, or near it):

> Margaret, are you grieving
> Over Goldengrove unleaving?

Disorder is present in two forms: in the child's weeping and in the fall and decay of the autumn leaves. No sooner does disorder appear than Hopkins's ordering impulses rush forward to cope with it:

> Ah! as the heart grows older
> It will come to such sights colder
> By and by, nor spare a sigh
> Though worlds of wanwood leafmeal lie;
>
> (lines 5–8)

These lines are an ordering response that attempts to control the disordering otherness of the child's grief. Paraphrased roughly, they say: you'll get used to it as you get older. The tone here verges on smugness; the speaker is telling her, instructing her, but he is also condescending to her. Smugness is the tonal giveaway of any poem where the ordering outweighs the disordering.

And here Hopkins's genius asserts itself: the child interrupts Father Hopkins's little disquisition with her urgency. Her dramatic otherness bursts his formal bubble:

> And yet you will weep and know why.
>
> (line 9)

His extra stress on "will" is just right—the child's feelings cannot be bought off or silenced by glib intimidation. The highly organized fifteen-line "sonnet" pivots here at its triple-rhymed center, pivots on its syntax ("And yet"), and pauses heavily as line and meaning unit are coincident for the first time in the poem. In addition, the key thematic word "why" culminates a cluster of end rhymes and internal rhymes. "Why." This single line, and the dramatic opposition it presents to the poem's initial ordering principles, hurts the speaker to a deeper level of engagement with the themes at the same time that it asserts the imperative of authentic feeling. The poem's preliminary ordering, a false ordering, a human controlling ordering (like that of a dismissive parent) gives way before the child's insistent, instructive grief.

The poem, through this single line, dramatizes another dimension of the poem's greatness: the disparity between secular orderings and sacred orderings. The worldly and worldly-wise "understanding" of human nature and experience the speaker exemplifies in lines 5 through 8 only satisfy *his* needs. But the child's needs, the needs of deep grief, can only be understood in relation to a sacred ordering that brings human innerness into play—what the heart has heard of, ghost has guessed.

Only a sacred order can explain her sorrow, can place her tears in an ordering context. The sacred ordering Hopkins proposes is the Christian myth of the Fall of Man through original sin, which brought death into the world. Since this myth presupposes God's complete and total ordering of the world since its beginning, it can subsume Margaret's individual grief at a deep enough level—scoop it up, roots and all, not just blossom, carry if off toward that future in which she will be transplanted in heaven's garden, beyond all ill. Yet it seems to me that the same language also expresses a pagan ordering which is equally convincing (and thus consoling): you, Margaret, are a part of this timebound, natural world; you intuit your own death in the falling of leaves because of the mystical unity of all life. This pagan ordering is tragic at the personal level, but its consoling power is equally profound or a poem like Whitman's "Crossing Brooklyn Ferry" could not move us as it does.

The two endings call for a slight difference in tone. The Christian version has Father Hopkins back in the saddle—it's a homily, a deep homily directed at the child. The other, the pagan version, has more feeling for the rightness of her grief, and the repetition of her name in the final line makes her individual identity a part of the universal order. To me, there's enough of Whitman still unexpurgated in Hopkins's imagination to make this second reading equally believable.

But, to return to my earlier assertion, in either poem (the pagan or the Christian), it is the child's presence that turns the poem away from the self-enclosed certainties, it is the disorder of her interruption ("And yet you will weep and know why") that lets a deeper order in.

The nature of the disorder in a poem tells us what the poet's human concerns are. The orders he discovers, creates, or imposes to respond to that disorder are his gift to the human community—a representative manifestation of the human encounter with disorder and a possible response to it. What makes Hopkins's poem important is that he is able to take on two disorderings: the universal disorder of death/decay and the immediate dramatic disorder of personal emotional demand on the self. Both challenge his ordering impulse, the child's grief especially, pushing his poem past its easy answers to a vision of a deeper order more adequate to the deep disorder the child has glimpsed.

Order and Disorder in Lyric Poetry

Art must insist on interpretations that are germane to its essence.
—Nietzsche, *The Birth of Tragedy*

This power [of imagination] . . . reveals itself in the balance or reconciliation of opposite or discordant qualities: . . . a more than usual state of emotion, with more than usual order.
—Coleridge, *Biographia Literaria*

When Coleridge says that to ask "what is poetry" is almost the same as asking "what is a poet," he is linking the psychology of making to the product made. In this essay I'll move quite easily between poet and poem because I think that Coleridge's list of balanced or reconciled opposites contains one pair ("a more than usual state of emotion, with more than usual order") which is in fact an essence, though I prefer the terms "disorder" and "order."

I think of poetry as an alternate world, one which the poet creates out of language in order to tell important stories about being human. The esthetic essence that is germane to that alternate world is an interplay of order and disorder. The reality of disorder and the human need for order assert themselves in the enclosed world of the poem. According to this understanding, one goal of the poem is to manifest both disorder and order in a dynamic tension that gives us a compelling picture of the world: the truth of its disorder (the role of chance, accident, randomness) and the need for order. The particular form these two forces take in the poem, their proportional presence, and the dynamic relationship between them constitute, in large part, a particular poet's vision.

It could be said that poets are first attracted to poetry be-

---

Written in 1989.

cause they are simultaneously highly aware of disorder (either within themselves or in the world) and of poetry's cultural role as a huge repository of such powerful formal ordering principles as rhyme, meter, stanza pattern, incantatory repetition, syntactical parallelism, symbol, and those principles of story structure analyzed by Aristotle in his *Poetics*. The young poet brings her disorder (thematic) to Poetry's order (formal) in order that the two will form a larger whole in which both are compellingly present. From that naive but authentic beginning more complex relationships of order and disorder emerge.

If poetry provides numerous formal ordering principles, then life itself provides the disorder that is the raw material of poetry. Whether we are aware of it as chance, accident, or randomness, disorder is omnipresent in the world of experience. Though ordering principles can be both formal and thematic in poetry, disorder is most likely to manifest itself as theme. If Love and Death are the great themes of lyric poetry, we can see that, though they function differently in the work of different poets, they appear first and primarily as disorder. Now, in the post-Romantic, individualist West we regard Love as as one of a very few available ordering principles, but that may be only after it is transformed by art. Certainly the Greeks saw passionate love as a form of madness, one that could easily lead to the savage disasters perpetrated by Medea in her hopeless love of and rage at Jason. Or consider Sappho—the very source of the personal, passionate lyric constantly tormented by love and desire. And the Troubadour poets of the twelfth century, first formulating our ennobling and ordering principles of romantic love, did their best to insinuate disorder into the formula by insisting that such love be hopeless and illicit.

To the extent that the human ordering response is the act of creating meaning when inspired by the assertion of disorder, then Death is the Great Disorder, the great negator of meanings against which all orderings in some way respond. I have long felt that in the silences between words and the pauses between lines in a lyric poem, one can hear the faintly whispered refrain "we are mortal." Whether the death is a loved one's or the prospect of one's own, whenever the theme is introduced into a poem it must call forth an ordering principle.

On the other hand, it would be a great mistake to conclude that disorder is simply destructive. In fact, disorder can be a vitalizing element in the interplay of disorder and order, as in Herrick's "Delight in Disorder," where the rhymed couplets and constraints of costume are resisted by a seductive disarray of "erring lace" and "cuff neglectful," only to be reconciled and celebrated in the formula of "wild civility." Or, on a more serious level, there is the disorder called risk, in which the individual must push beyond security to discover the unknown. As Baudelaire urges in the final lines of "Le Voyage": "Plonger au fond du gouffre, Enfer ou Ciel, qu'importe? / Au fond de l'Inconnu pour trouver du nouveau!" (. . . into the gulf's depths, whether it's heaven or hell, what matter? / into the Unknown in quest of something new!). Or as the suddenly frightened, then reinvigorated speaker of D. H. Lawrence's "Song of a Man Who Has Come Through" concludes:

> What is the knocking? What is the knocking in the night?
> It is somebody wants to do us harm.
> No, no, it is the three strange angels. Admit them, admit them.

Order and Disorder: A Brief Example

Let me give an example of how we might consider a poem as an interplay of orderings and disorderings and, in tracing this interplay, uncover that place where the humanly compelling and the esthetic intersect. Here is a brief poem of Keats's often known as "Lines Supposed to Have Been Addressed to Fanny Brawne":

> This living hand, now warm and capable
> Of earnest grasping, would, if it were cold
> And in the icy silence of the tomb,
> So haunt thy days and chill thy dreaming nights
> That thou wouldst wish thine own heart dry of blood
> So in my veins red life might stream again
> And thou be conscience-calm'd—See here it is—
> I hold it towards you.

How might we consider the kinds of order and disorder that create a dramatic unity out of these eight lines? The first ordering principle that comes to mind is that of thematic tradition: it is a poem of seduction, melancholy cousin of Marvell's "To His Coy Mistress" and numerous others of that ilk. As a seduction poem, its structure and especially its resolution are predetermined—the charming (in a double sense) imaginative logic of the speaker will compel the lady to yield her favors. Within the order of that tradition, Keats's poem is disordered by the content or theme of his argument. No jaunty, self-assured wit here as one might find in Herrick or Marvell, but a passionate, morbid, sensual urgency. There is frequently an opportunistic quality about poems in the carpe diem tradition, a sense that the speaker (and it is almost always a he) is using the threat of time's passing mostly because he thinks it will work. In this sense the carpe diem poem can seem superficial because the speaker frequently seems above the implications of his own argument, immune to the deep disorder implied by time's passing and earthly uncertainty. Not so Keats. This is no ploy with him; he is as haunted and tortured by it as his addressee.

Keats's basic rhetorical strategy is guilt inducement. If we were to paraphrase the poem's morbid and diabolical logic it might unfold like this: "I'm here and available, but if/when I'm dead you'll feel so guilty you'll become obsessed; day and night you'll know no peace of mind until you'll be driven to the brink of suicide yourself, where you'll vainly hope that by killing yourself you can raise me from the dead and thus be released from the psychological agony. But (and here disorder yields to order) luckily all this can be avoided: I'm still here and you can take this opportunity to love me here and now while we're both alive." As if this content were not disordered and baroque enough, let me add that its intent is disordering: it means to conjure up fear and terror. Two deaths are invoked as probabilities or possibilities: the poet's own and the addressee's. You could even say that two deaths are threatened, and madness as well. This is strong manipulation and goes way beyond that social set piece: the soldier leaving for the front presenting his last, strongest argument to his resistant sweetheart. Here, the speaker is manipulatively threatening about his own death and her consequent guilt, which might sap her of the desire to live—but these disorders, though he is utilizing them in a seduction poem, represent genuine, deep disorders and threats to human beings in general. To seize the moment, seize fast to another human being against the (perpetual) imminence of death, is an important, compelling possibility.

But there are other kinds of order and disorder in this poem. At the very moment the poem enters the thematic disorder of its argument, it adopts a formal ordering device of elaborately balanced clauses and paired phrasings. This rhetorical syntax is reassuringly elevated in tone, even as its enumeration of night and day is indicating that the threat is absolute, incessant, inescapable: "So haunt thy days and chill thy dreaming nights." This ordering rhetoric perfectly coincides with the most threatening content, so that when, in the last one-and-a-half lines, the threat is burst, the whole "haunting" exposed as no more than a hypothetical threat, the rhetorical bubble is also burst by a sudden shift to direct gestural speech:

> See here it is—
> I hold it towards you.

Tone shifts, diction shifts, most of all, syntax shifts abruptly, powerfully from the balanced clauses of formal argument to the direct simplicity of urgent speech. We have, in quick succession, an imperative, a presentation: "here it is," and a movement toward the hearer (and reader): "I hold it towards you." The word is the thing; the image of a hand that frames the poem has been transformed from the passive potential of line one to the startling, active gesture of the final line.

Put another way, the rhetoric, the elaborate syntax, and the quirky story that take over after line one are meant to disorder and disorient the recipient, so that when the hand appears at poem's end it appears to rescue her from the deep water the poem has plunged her into. The hand at the beginning of the poem returns at the end to reassert the poem's main sustaining order: passionate bodily presence in the moment. Keats has taken the "carpe diem" concept (which has ordered poems since Horace and sustained humans for who knows how long) and given it the anguish and urgent disorder of his own obsessions with death, loss, and sensuality. That the poem compels and moves us now is a tribute not to its inherited order, but to the tension between that order and the terrifying disorder Keats brings out of himself to place against it.

Syntax: An Ambiguous or "Situational" Technique of Order in Poetry

The example of the Keats poem "Lines Supposed to Have Been Addressed to Fanny Brawne" is one in which an obvious thematic disorder is answered by formal and thematic ordering principles. In thinking about the interplay of order and disorder in a particular poem, it is useful to think in terms of formal disordering as well. For example, syntax as defined by the *Random House College Dictionary* is "the pattern and structure of the word order in a sentence or phrase." Since, in written language, syntax is the primary regulator and orderer of meaning, it would seem logical that in poetry it almost always functions as a formal ordering principle.

In the poetry of certain cultures this is true to the point that they utilize patterns of syntax much the way other cultures use meter and rhyme, as a fundamental, defining structural device. Chinese *shih* (lyric) poetry of the T'ang dynasty required not only a set number of characters per line and a set number of lines (eight), but also that the four lines in the middle form couplets that were syntactically parallel even as they were conceptually and tonally contrasting if not antithetical:

A Traveler at Night Writes His Thoughts

Delicate grasses, faint wind on the bank;
stark mast, a long night boat:
stars hang down, over broad fields sweeping;
the moon boils up, on the great river flowing.
Fame—how can my writings win me that?
Office—age and sickness have brought it to an end.

> Fluttering, fluttering—where is my likeness?
> Sky and earth and one sandy gull.
>
> (Tu Fu, eighth century)

Hebrew poetry of the Psalms likewise relies on the formal principle of several sorts of syntactical parallelism rather than on rhyme or meter.

Perhaps an extreme of the ordering perception of syntax in English was articulated by Ernest Fenollosa when he claimed that the transitive sentence characteristic of both Chinese poetry and English grammatical structure "was forced upon primitive men by nature itself" and was "a reflection of the temporal order in causation." He seemed to perceive an almost mystical correspondence between transitive syntax and the scientific ordering principle of cause and effect:

> It seems to me that the normal and typical sentence in English as well as in Chinese expresses just this unit of natural process. It consists of three necessary words: the first denoting the agent or subject from which the act starts, the second embodying the very stroke of the act, the third pointing to the object, the receiver of the impact. Thus:
> Farmer   pounds   rice
> This brings language close to *things,* and in its strong reliance upon verbs it erects all speech into a kind of dramatic poetry.
> (*The Chinese Written Character as a Medium for Poetry*)

But, within the overall order of a grammatical sentence, syntax has an enormous potential for adding to the disordered aspect of the poem as well. Few poets have explored or exploited this disordering potential of syntax in English more effectively than Yeats, who related it directly to the major breakthrough that occurred in his work around 1916:

> I began to make it [a language to my liking] when I discovered some twenty years ago that I must seek, not as Wordsworth thought, words in common use, but a powerful and passionate syntax, and a complete coincidence between period and stanza. Because I need a passionate syntax for passionate subject matter I compel myself to accept those traditional metres that have

developed with the language. ("A General Introduction to My Work," 1937)

Yeats immediately counters the expressive disordering power of syntax with the formal ordering of traditional stanzas and meters, instinctively sensing that their dynamic interplay is central to his poems.

That "passion" is disordering is an essential theme of Yeats's work, whether it be love's passion or the political passions that constantly rend his homeland. (Think of the connection between cleanliness and order and then consider Yeats's famous image for the emotional life: "the foul rag and bone shop of the heart.")

Frequently, his syntax calls for elaborate suspensions of meaning:

> No handiwork of Callimachus,
> Who handled marble as if it were bronze,
> Made draperies that seemed to rise
> When sea-wind swept the corner, stands
>
> ("Lapis Lazuli")

Although here the sound echo of subject, "handiwork," and predicate, "stands," helps to bridge the clausal distance.

Or the lines sometimes unfold so cryptically that the feeling arrives before or almost in spite of the meaning that should be revealed by the syntax, as in, for example, the final stanza of "Crazy Jane and Jack the Journeyman," where she speaks of her dead lover:

> But were I left to lie alone
> In an empty bed,
> The skein so bound us ghost to ghost
> When he turned his head
> Passing on the road that night,
> Mine must walk when dead.

From the contortions of Yeats to the dislocations of Hopkins or the deeper entanglements of Hart Crane is a journey toward the more profound disordering possibilities of syntax.

If syntax is guide and guardian of a sentence's logic, then Crane's ambition to articulate his age and his sensibility— "New conditions of life germinate new forms of spiritual articulation" ("General Aims and Theories," 1937)—called for "an apparent illogic [that] operates so logically in conjunction with its context in the poem as to establish its claim to another logic, quite independent of the original definition of the word or phrase or image thus employed" (letter to Harriet Monroe, 1926). His fascination with the ocean (poetry's primary concrete image for disorder), his assertion that "language has built towers and bridges, but itself is inevitably as fluid as always" ("General Aims and Theories")—do these notions and preoccupations authorize his eccentric expressive efforts with syntax? Sometimes the simpler dislocations have simple explanations. The inversions of the first sentence of "At Melville's Tomb" allow him to have two meanings:

> Often beneath the wave, wide from this ledge
> The dice of drowned men's bones he saw bequeath
> An embassy.

Wishing to keep a grip on meaning, and feeling the pressure of clause piled on clause, the reader's mind completes the sentence by seizing the probable subject at the first opportunity and getting "Often he saw the dice of drowned men's bones." "Bequeath" breaks the sentence open again and is absorbed as "Often he saw the dice of drowned men's bones bequeath an embassy." But what happens when we step off the shore's ledge and give ourselves over to the unfettered leewardings of this passage, which opens section four of "Voyages"?

> Whose counted smile of hours and days, suppose
> I know as spectrum of the sea and pledge
> Vastly now parting gulf on gulf of wings
> Whose circles bridge, I know, (from palms to the severe
> Chilled albatross's white immutability)
> No stream of greater love advancing now
> Than, singing, this mortality alone
> Through clay aflow immortally to you.

Amen, we say. I'm not claiming it's immune to explication, nor that it is antisyntactical, but that we are experiencing an extremely expressive use of syntax, one that mocks the skeletal parsing of sentence with an image of fleshly, ecstatic flowing, one that disorders syntax in the service of theme.

My point is simply this: syntax can function along the entire continuum from order to disorder, starting from the straightforward simplicity of the transitive sentence and extending to the passionate expressiveness of Yeats, and further toward the vitalizing or bewildering disorder of much of Hart Crane's work.

Disorder and Order in Poetry

To love a poet is not simply to find his or her order satisfying and convincing; it is also to find his or her disorder genuinely threatening, or, at the very least, significantly disturbing. What threatens us? What order convinces and reassures us? These senses of threat and order are among the most personal, the most subjective of all assessments. They are fundamental to our whole being—to the structures of our personalities, to the way we live our lives. A product of our temperament and the formative circumstances of our lives, they do not originate in poetry or any other art form, but they do, constantly and consistently, extend from our lived lives into our judgments about poetry.

What is threatening to one person is not so to another. Or the degree of threat is at issue—a threshold must be crossed. Or the form of expression affects the sense of threat. Likewise with ordering. What is a deeply felt ordering principle to one person may seem mechanical to another (as with many free verse versus formalist arguments). Or what seems adequate order to one person will seem a dam about to burst, a house about to collapse, or rampant barbarism to another. One person's well-wrought urn is another's airless tomb and he says with Whitman, "Unscrew the locks from the doors! / Unscrew the doors themselves from their jambs!"

Many people I know feel deeply uncomfortable or repelled

by the later poetry of Sylvia Plath, and I think in large part because the disorder and violence seem far stronger than the ordering principles. No use to say that "Lady Lazarus" uses story, rhyme, internal rhyme, short lines end-stopped—all to order the disorder of rage and malevolent revenge that is alternately enthralling and menacing. To say, as these people do of Plath, that someone is "hysterical" is to say that his or her emotions are beyond control or structure. And the issues of disorder and order are not merely esthetic judgments, but quickly shade over into moral judgments as well, because we feel that the principles of our own being are at stake, and so we soon find ourselves becoming defensive and making large claims about this or that poem or poet in order to mask our more subjective personal claims.

An Autobiographical Digression

Since it seems to me that one's relationship to disorder and order is determined primarily by temperament and the circumstances of one's life, I think it's incumbent on me to make a brief autobiographical digression that might establish the origins and nature of my own response to the issues.

If disorder's fiercest face is random, life-threatening violence, then my own experience of it would be my younger brother's death in a hunting accident when I was twelve. Since I was holding the gun that killed him, the horror of the event entered me as a participant as well as witness. Wishing, no doubt, to console me for what I had done and to explain the universe to themselves as well, several adults came to my room the evening of his death and earnestly and compassionately informed me that it was an accident. Accident. Interesting word. It is with words that we try to make order, that I even now am trying to make order and coherence. The word "accident" to a twelve-year-old's mind was the true name of terror. Is this a world ruled by accident? Are accidents of the sort that leave your younger brother a lifeless corpse at your feet—are these things just part of what the world is about? Unbearable word, unbearable world—this accident. My twelve-year-old mind knew instinctively it couldn't survive by such a concept as accident and went quickly to work trying to impose order, which is meaning, on this horror. I had heard about good and evil—like everyone else, I sensed them in myself. But here was an eight-year-old boy—dead. He was my brother; he was innocent and good. And he was dead. If good was dead, then evil must have done it, and so I was evil. What little religious background I had gave me the story of Cain and Abel, and the story seemed to fit enough to do the job, to restore order and meaning, and thus it was assimilated into the explanation I was formulating. So, as a youngster I had a near-fatal dose of the amoral, nameless, random horror that sometimes surfaces in human lives. I instinctively rejected that understanding of it called "accident" as partaking of the horror, not mitigating it in any way, not making it possible for me to integrate the experience into an ongoing life. And, unimpressed and unconsoled by the ordering principles that adults offered, I formulated my own rigid ordering principle of good and evil, Abel and Cain.

I have no wish to dwell on this story. It's enough to say that I experienced what I think all must feel, certainly all poets: a personal instance of the threat of disorder and a personal discovery of the mind's ability to, need to, create or discover an ordering principle to counter the threat and permit life to continue. How prevalent and intense the documented disorder in poets' lives. How many poets orphaned at an early age. How many with violent or alcoholic parents. How many people who can read Roethke's "My Papa's Waltz" with a full sense of the child's terror and awe against which the poem's formal structure, the very metaphor of the waltz itself, must assert its calming, ordering powers.

Two Anecdotes about Masks

What Picasso asserted in 1930 about a Nimba fertility goddess mask that hung outside his studio might well stand as another instance of the interplay of disorder and order in art:

> Men had made these masks ... for a sacred purpose, a magic purpose, as a kind of mediation between themselves and the unknown hostile forces that surrounded them in order to overcome their fear and horror by giving it a form and an image. At that moment [1907 or 1908], I realized what painting was all about. Painting isn't an esthetic operation; it's a form of magic designed as a mediation between this strange, hostile world and us, a way of seizing power by giving form to our terrors as well as our desires. When I came to this realization, I knew I had found my way. (Françoise Gilot, *My Life with Picasso*)

The key term may not be "power," the psychological reward you feel when your ordering principle is in place. The key phrase may be "mediating"—the ordering principle doesn't triumph over or obliterate what Picasso calls "the unknown hostile forces"; it mediates between them and the self.

Consider another anecdote about masks. Among the Iroquois tribes, the fiercest supernatural creatures were called "flying heads"—demons in the form of disembodied heads zooming at night among the trees, their faces distorted with the anguish of evil and malice. If you saw one in a dream, you had to go into the woods, carve its features on a living basswood tree, and then, with appropriate rituals, cut down the tree, take the carved section home, and complete the

---

Written in 1988.

mask. Donning the mask in False Face ceremonies, you became your own demon and had the power to cure certain diseases. If you failed to respond to the dream, you would yourself sicken and die.

The Iroquois were a traditional society, one of whose hallmarks was a shared dream theory which, among other things, could help to alleviate the burden of personal confusion for the dreamer. Beyond that, the anecdote speaks of rituals and a social institution (the False Face Society) that integrated a personal, subjective experience of disorder into a framework of social order. But by Picasso's time, Western society was too fragmented for such culturewide integration and the individual tended to be left to his or her own devices when it came to responding to disorder, whether such disorder was internal to the self or external. Artists, especially poets, in post-traditional society are particularly attuned to this situation—their art form becomes the arena for the contest, the agon, between disorder and order. Later, they present the completed art work to the culture as something that resolves or holds in tension a disorder and order which, if the art is important, is both individual and representative of the culture at large.

Picasso gives us insight into the magical nature of the artistic enterprise. The Iroquois give us a dynamic image of the personal healing (and urgency or risk) involved in the making of a magical mask. If Picasso gives us an image of the artist in post-traditional Western society, seeking his way, uncertain of his or his art's deeper purposes until some personal discovery takes place, then the Iroquois provide an image of how such a mask-maker might move out, through drama and social institutions, into a significant relationship with the surrounding society. In the Iroquois story we see the healing effects of drama, both on the mask-maker (the poet) and on the tribe (the audience).

II

Lyric to Dramatic Lyric

Keats and Yeats
From Lyric to Dramatic Lyric

The waking have one world in common; sleepers have each a private world of his own.
—Heraclitus, fragment 15 (trans. Wheelwright)

Both Keats and Yeats are tempted to retreat into their private worlds as dreamers. Both need the transcendent; both fear the conditional world. To the early Keats of "Sleep and Poetry" (1816), the timebound world was a "muddy stream" of "real things" that threatened to "bear along / [his] soul to nothingness." To Yeats, as early drafts of "The Circus Animals' Desertion" show, it is "life" and not "the heart" that he calls a "foul rag and bone shop."

Both poets could easily have retreated into the pure lyric as dream. Neither did in their best work. Both moved outward (from different motives, toward different goals) from lyric to dramatic lyric—that is, from a passive self to a self able to dramatize its concerns in conflict and interaction with a larger world and the others who inhabit it.

For Keats, such a movement away from the self-enclosed early lyrics is therapeutic: the early lyrics are overwhelmed by the claustrophobic disorder of his emotions. When his poems succeed in locating an "other," some being outside himself (say, the bright star, the nightingale, Fanny Brawne), he is able, in the dramatic interaction, to clarify his own needs and desires and to order his being.

The younger Yeats, on the contrary, relished the self-enclosed nature of his early lyrics. Their lulling rhythms and

---

Delivered as a lecture at Warren Wilson College, 1991.

symbolic situations were intended to entrance readers so that they might contemplate a transcendent "divine order, divine beauty." In fact, these poems were too highly ordered; they feel hermetic and unreal. When the world finally enters Yeats's poems (especially as politics and history in "Easter 1916," but also as his discovery of "passionate syntax" at the same time), it brings a salutary and vitalizing disorder to the work.

My claim is not that this movement from lyric to dramatic lyric is the only significant one in either Keats or Yeats, nor that the work can or should be reduced to instances of the dramatic lyric. What I am contending is that the dramatic lyric is a form particularly suited to presenting a rich picture of the self in the world and that we can trace its qualities in the chronology of both poets' shorter lyrics. In the dramatic lyric, we have two truths powerfully present. We have the truth of the lyric: that the self longs for the unconditional, for a transcendence of suffering and mortality. And we have the truth of the world: that we are bound by time and space, that our bodies are mortal. In the full-fledged dramatic lyric these two truths contend in the arena of the unfolding poem.

Keats, whose preparation for living in the world consisted largely of training to become a physician, spent much of his brief life as a poet trying to determine if he was a healer or a patient, a poet of necessary ecstasies or a fevered dreamer. The dreamer is an ill creature—"thou art a dreaming thing / A fever of thy self," the goddess Moneta declares in *The Fall of Hyperion*. The poet, though also alienated from the world as it is, is a healer, "a physician to all men." When Keats asks, in the last lines of the "Ode to a Nightingale,"

> Was it a vision or a waking dream?
> Fled is that music. Do I wake or sleep?

he is continuing an anguished self-interrogation into the nature of his enterprise. To experience and, through the writing of poems, to bring back to others a vision is to "pour out a balm on all the world"; to dream is merely to poison one's own earthly existence and to "vex" that of others.

The line of distinction between the clan of dreamers and the clan of poets is not always clear, but it is certain that both differ radically from those who are reconciled to the world, who are "no dreamers weak; / They seek no wonder but the human face, / No music but a happy-noted voice" (*The Fall of Hyperion*). Keats's poets and dreamers, like his "wretched wight" who has gazed too long at the Faery lady in "La Belle Dame Sans Merci," are cut off from the world of process; seen through the world's eyes, they are "alone and palely loitering" among the autumnal woods.

To be unreconciled to the world's terms is a necessary precondition of the personal lyric. Put another way, the distinctive motive for the personal lyric is a longing for the unconditional. Keats's most succinct positive expression of that longing occurs in book 1 of *Endymion:*

> Wherein lies happiness? In that which becks
> Our ready minds to fellowship divine,
> A fellowship with essence; till we shine
> Full-alchemiz'd and free of space.
>
> (lines 777–80)

The inverse of this transcendent ecstasy is represented by this world as a place of suffering, mortality, and ephemeral joy:

> Here, where men sit and hear each other groan
> ("Ode to a Nightingale")

Suffering takes place in the world of time and space, on the horizontal axis of narrative. There is a vertical axis that rises by "gradations" toward happiness; Keats calls it a "kind of Pleasure Thermometer" (interestingly a medical metaphor). This vertical lyric axis exists at a 90-degree angle to the horizontal and is imagined to be outside time and space. These two coordinates map the struggles of the lyric self. In Keats's earlier work he is oriented almost entirely toward the vertical axis of longing for the unconditional—an axis that rises directly out of the fevered self. Later, he is able to break out of the self-enclosed world of the earliest lyrics and enter into a relationship with things in the world. This new relationship is never easy, always haunted by lyric longing, but it is a far more effective and complex dramatization of his situation, and one that allows him at last to connect with other people and recognize himself as a poet rather than a dreamer.

Keats must, in the phrase from Wordsworth's poem, "step forth into the light of things." "Things" will prove essential to Keats's growth as a poet, and the word itself recurs constantly and importantly throughout his work. The opening lines of *Endymion* assert that things of beauty transcend the conditions of human being:

> A thing of beauty is a joy forever

and provide the motive for poetry:

> Therefore, on every morrow, are we wreathing
> A flowery band to bind us to the earth.

These things (a bright star, an urn, a bird, even his beloved's anatomy) also represent existences outside the self—things that can break the self free of its fevered longings and self-enclosure and also act to bring it into relationship with the conditional world—to "bind [it] to the earth."

Things seldom reconcile Keats to the terms of this world, but they create a relationship between self and other, self and thing which allows him to dramatize the complexities and intensities of his situation. They allow him to move from the personal lyric's concern with self to a concern with self-in-the-world, from being to being-in-the-world.

But first "things" must appear in his poems, and they are scarce in his earliest lyrics. A reader might reasonably expect an early sonnet entitled "On Seeing the Elgin Marbles for the First Time" to be replete with objects and descriptive language, but "seeing" becomes, finally, ironic in a poem where the speaker's self is opaque—he himself is all the world there is and unhappy in it:

> My spirit is too weak; mortality
>   Weighs heavily on me like unwilling sleep,
>   And each imagin'd pinnacle and steep
> Of godlike hardship tells me I must die
> Like a sick eagle looking at the sky.
>   Yet 'tis a gentle luxury to weep,
>   That I have not the cloudy winds to keep
> Fresh for the opening of the morning's eye.
> Such dim-conceived glories of the brain
>   Bring round the heart an indescribable feud;
> So do these wonders a most dizzy pain,
>   That mingles Grecian grandeur with the rude
> Wasting of old Time—with a billowy main,
>   A sun, a shadow of a magnitude.
>
>   (1817)

The poet's gaze is not directed outward at all, but inward toward an interior landscape where the only physical objects, the only nouns in the poem, are emblems for his self and his situation in the oppressive conditional world. The eagle is "sick" and thus confined in this world rather than soaring above it as its nature warrants and its longing demands. In the entire poem, there isn't a single descriptive reference to the Parthenon friezes or their content. Even the vaguely evoked "Grecian grandeur" exists simply as a symptom of the poet's soul-sickness, his "most dizzy pain."

In this self-enclosed and claustrophobic early lyric, one can feel the true burden of sensibility in Keats. Keats is someone who feels intensely and obscurely; a volatile personality who experiences his passions passively—more as their victim than their source. When his early lyrics center in the self and its emotions, the theme of the poem will be one of anguished disorder, often imaged as disease and fever (a tracing of the occurrence of "ache" would reveal a lot). The self-enclosing impulses of the lyric are a curse for Keats's personality—though he longs for the sky, for "aetherial" things, he experiences most vividly their lack or his failure to reach them.

What will rescue Keats from the disorder of his own feelings is the appearance of separately existing objects in his poems—things set off from the "I" of the poem. In the interplay of identification with or longing for these other things, Keats can organize and dramatize his story. Thus, the enormous clarity and dramatic power when, a year after the Elgin marbles sonnet, he is able to postulate an other, a thing—the "bright star" of this sonnet:

> Bright star, would I were stedfast as thou art—
>   Not in lone splendour hung aloft the night
> And watching, with eternal lids apart,
>   Like Nature's patient, sleepless Eremite,
> The moving waters at their priestlike task
>   Of pure ablution round earth's human shores,
> Or gazing on the new soft-fallen mask
>   Of snow upon the mountains and the moors—
> No—yet still stedfast, still unchangeable,
>   Pillow'd upon my fair love's ripening breast,
> To feel for ever its soft fall and swell,
>   Awake for ever in a sweet unrest,
> Still, still to hear her tender-taken breath,
> And so live ever—or else swoon to death.
>   (November 1818)

When there are two centers of energy in a poem, then there is the disharmony or conflict that must be present for drama to take place. Here we have the "bright star" and the "I." We also have the external landscape of the "mountains and the moors"—a distant and distinct landscape that will suddenly become intimate and warm as it metamorphoses in line 10 into the sensuous terrain of the beloved's anatomy. The poem's drama is one of distances and their collapse; and of the persistence of an absolute ideal ("stedfast and unchangeable") that shows the speaker's loyalties are to the unconditional world even as his equally strong urge is that the unconditional become incarnated in the conditional world.

In this version of the lyric self, the imagination agrees to flee from its own internal, subjective emotions only if it can achieve an identity beyond process, beyond change. Its simultaneous wish is to be transformed beyond the conditions of this world and yet to have this transformed state charged with intensity of sensuous feeling (not the distant, unmoved star, but something else).

That something else is Keats's particular contribution to the aspirations of the lyric self: he proposes a moment of sensual arousal suspended forever, yet filled with intense emotion. It is the precoital bliss he celebrates in the figures of the painted lovers on the Grecian urn, a pair of bodies frozen in gestures of desire, a kind of apogee of arousal that is immune to the consequences of action in time—the consummation that leads to postcoital symptoms as "a heart high-sorrowful and cloy'd / A burning forehead, and a parching tongue." To return to the terms of "Bright Star"—not an ascetic hermit, not a mask (beautiful, but covering the face), but instead, a sensual though chaste lover and a bared breast: an intimacy that partakes of this world of process and flux, though only in that one word "ripening" that leaps out with its long "i," its harsh initial "r."

Failing to achieve his impossible longing—to be "like" the star in certain absolute qualities, but not condemned to such detachment and ascetic (esthetic?) distance from the sensual world—failing to achieve something related to ascent on the vertical lyric axis, the speaker is willing and eager to descend this lyric axis toward its negative pole—to swoon to death.

Stylistically, the sonnet's sestet generates and sustains its lyric aspiration through a rich texture of sound patterns distinct from those of the octet. These include the incantatory repetition of key thematic words, especially the word "still," whose repetition in lines 9 and then in line 13 acts to encapsulate the suspended moment it also evokes in its pun on "stillness." Likewise, the key term "for ever" appears twice and climaxes the moment as "ever" in line 14. The sestet is full of consonantal repetitions, especially "f," "s," and "l" sounds, notably line 11 ("to feel for ever its soft fall and swell") where the consonants are interwoven with varying vowels. If this rich texture of consonants and incantatory repetition surrounds the moment it creates, then line 14, which signals a breaking away from the stillness, picks up one of the octet's

47

patterns of vowel music when "swoon" harks back to "moving," "ablution," "human" and "new."

No doubt this bright star shone first in Shakespeare's sonnet 116, where it also exerted its organizing and orienting powers: "[Love] is an ever-fixèd mark / . . . It is the star to every wand'ring bark." But it is crucial to note that in Keats's sonnet it is the thingness, the starness, that is primary, not the abstraction called "love."

Turning to its date of composition, we note that it was written around the time he first met Fanny Brawne—in other words, a moment when the lyric self has just been powerfully awakened to a desirable otherness in the world. Even though "Bright Star" seems to be a poem in which the lyric self and its needs for transcendence dominate (the star gets eight lines, the relationship to the beloved only four), we can already feel the pressure of the world and the world's reality against the self.

Keats's remarkable growth as a poet is paralleled, traced, and anticipated in his letters, where he eloquently articulates his ideas and attitudes about poetry. In a letter of April 21, 1819, written around the same time as most of the great odes, he declares this timebound world to be a "vale of soul-making," not some way station to a Christian heaven. While we are here, three entities (heart, mind, and the world) act on each other to create our souls. In particular, a "World of Pains and troubles [is necessary] to school an intelligence and make it a soul." The very notion of life's task as the creation of a soul implies a major reconciliation of the self with the conditional world—everything then moves toward the story of action and reaction and interaction, toward, on the esthetic plane, the dramatic lyric.

One way of understanding "Ode to a Nightingale" is that the self is being schooled by the world—permitted to indulge its longing for the lyric world (ecstatic transcendence), but shown the limits of that transcendence. Permitted to rise above the world, but only part way, to the "verdurous glooms and winding mossy ways," not to the level of those entirely lyric beings, "the Queen-Moon" and "her starry Fays."

We might also look at "Ode to a Nightingale" in terms of the appearance of the "other" object, in this case, the bird. As with his earliest, most self-enclosed lyrics, the poem opens with a characteristic assertion of the primacy of the self's feelings and opinions:

> My heart aches, and a drowsy numbness pains
>   My sense, as though of hemlock I had drunk;
> Or emptied some dull opiate to the drains
>   One minute past, and Lethe-wards had sunk:
> 'Tis not through envy of thy happy lot,
>   But being too happy in thine happiness,
>   That thou, light-winged Dryad of the trees . . .

In fact, the bird doesn't even appear until line seven, and then it is not as a bird but as a "light-winged Dryad." Our lyric poet is still unreconciled to the world's reality, still reluctant to call a thing by its rightful name and thus credit nouns with their full power to summon the things of the world. Or conversely, still reluctant to credit the world, by way of its nouns, with the power to summon the self.

And yet, the striking thing about Keats's "Ode to a Nightingale" is the enormous growth it shows in terms of how much the lyric self can encounter in the world *without* betraying its lyric nature. This poem is a marvelously complex example of the dramatic lyric, because of the number of issues it engages and dramatizes. These include the self's encounter with its own desire for emotional intensity and for escape (ecstatic transcendence); its acknowledgment of the tools that culture provides for those escapes (drugs, alcohol, imagination); the location and articulation of the motives for transcendence (we live in a world of suffering, death, loss); the self's desire for annihilation as a form of transcendence or relief from pain ("Fade far away, dissolve . . ."); the role of imagination in transcendence (the unfortunate phrase "viewless wings of Poesy"); the self's accomplishment of the transcendence it aspires to ("Already with thee!"—the phrase that announces the self's transport); its consideration of the consequences of such transcendence ("I cannot see what flowers are at my feet"); the connection between ecstatic transcendence and the wish to die ("Darkling, I listen") and the drawbacks ("To thy high requiem become a sod"); the degrees or levels of transcendence (from "emperor and clown" to "Ruth" to "Faery lands"). And then, the pivot point of the poem, the word "forlorn," where the self reaches its apogee and crashes down into the time-bound world again, dramatizing the brief nature of such transcendent ecstasies. And finally, the consideration of the nature of the experience, whether it is a delusive dream or a vision of an important truth.

There are interesting parallels between the basic movement of the nightingale ode and the two-staged "mystical process of unselving" articulated by Nietzsche in *The Birth of Tragedy*. The notion of the artist's "unselving" has obvious relevance to Keats who, when a sparrow landed on his sill, liked nothing more than to "take part in its existence and pick about the Gravel" and who constantly sought "Richer entanglements, enthralments far / More self-destroying" (*Endymion*). According to Nietzsche, the Dionysian artist, under the power of music (as is Keats in this ode), is returned to the "eternal ground of being" which is universal suffering ("where we sit and hear each other groan"). This descent must necessarily precede the artist's redemption through transcendent identification with an Apollonian, unitary "dream-image" (the nightingale; "Already with thee!"). Though Nietzsche's concepts are intriguingly apt to Keats's poem, they differ in an essential respect—the philosopher's descent and subsequent ascent would leave us entirely in the world of lyric transcendence and idealization. The dramatic action of Keats's ode creates a parabola of transcendence—he begins on earth, oppressed by the conditional world, he transcends it, and then (most painful of messages the world gives the self) he falls back to earth and his existential aloneness, summoned by the word "forlorn"—the same death-knell of mortality Donne heard in his sonnet that begins "Ask not for whom the bell tolls / It tolls for thee."

The best model for this crucial movement, the self's fall away from the transcendent moment, is a brief passage in Keats's "Epistle to John Hamilton Reynolds" on the limits of imagination:

> Things cannot to the will
> Be settled, but they tease us out of thought;
> Or is it that imagination brought
> Beyond its proper bound, yet still confin'd,
> Lost in a sort of Purgatory blind,
> Cannot refer to any standard law
> Of either earth or heaven? It is a flaw
> In happiness, to see beyond our bourn—
> It forces us in summer skies to mourn,
> It spoils the singing of the Nightingale.
>
> (lines 76–85)

In the nightingale ode, when Keats is "with the bird" among the trees, "lost in a sort of Purgatory blind," he engages in two imaginative motions. One is outward from his body into the "embalmed darkness" where he "guesses" at what sensory objects surround him; the other motion follows the bird's music as it leads further and further away from his conditional moment. First it leads to history (time has been abolished and social distinctions as well, both "emperor and clown" are nourished by the song), then to the semi-history of biblical tale or legend, then finally to a vision of Romance that exists entirely outside the conditions of human being (magic casements . . .). It is this overreaching, this aspiring to the Queen-Moon and all her starry fays, that causes his crashing earthward on the word "forlorn." What Nietzsche's Apollonian artist would accomplish, Keats recognizes as a reaching "beyond our bourn." What's more, the psychological accuracy, the "truth," is with Keats's model of transcendence—whether it be drugs, alcohol, imagination, or (in other poems) sex, we know transcendence to be a brief arc and a hard landing.

Once the poet has returned to earth, the world takes over and the bird, birdlike and no dryad now, flies across a worldly landscape: "Past the near meadows, over the still stream, / Up the hill-side," leaving the poet to pose his question about the reality and value of his experience.

Stylistically, Keats's movement from lyric to dramatic lyric involves numerous shifts of emphasis. Most notably, his diction

51

shifts away from Latinate polysyllables toward monosyllables derived from the Anglo-Saxon sources of English. Such a shift brings with it thickened consonant clusters, more varied vowels, and heightened stressing, all of which create a more sensuous sound and rhythmic texture. Nowhere is this more obvious than in "To Autumn," that hymn to the conditional world of ripeness and rot where the self has achieved its annihilation and been utterly assimilated into creatures, landscape, and song. But even when Latinate language is retained, it is far more likely to be dramatized. We can compare the relative inertness of this line from the first sonnet we examined:

> mortality
> Weighs heavily upon me like unwilling sleep

with a thematically similar line from the nightingale ode:

> No hungry generations tread thee down.

In the latter, the thick sound and physical intensity of the verb "tread" and the heavy stressing of the last three syllables anchor the Latinate "generations" and catch the line up into dramatized gesture.

There is also a noticeable shift away from a heavy reliance on adjectives, potentially the most passive part of speech, especially when they are atmospheric, as many are in early Keats. When Keats indulges his pleasure in adjectives in the later work, they are likely to become an assertion of the sensuous presence of the conditional world. And when adjectives become linked, in the later dramatic lyrics, to obsessive themes, they can acquire a startling rhythmic authority and power to dramatize a fixation, say, mortality:

> a few, sad, last gray hairs
> ("Ode to a Nightingale")

or sensuality:

> That warm, white, lucent, million-pleasured breast.
> ("To Fanny")

In both instances the adjectives make palpable the anguish of terror or desire as they cling to nouns of anatomy, emblems of the mortal human condition.

Our earlier discussion of Keats's development has emphasized the emergence of concrete, particular nouns as a sign of the presence of an other in the poems. The role of verbs in dramatic gesture becomes apparent in the remarkable late poem usually called "Lines Supposed to Have Been Addressed to Fanny Brawne":

> This living hand, now warm and capable
> Of earnest grasping, would, if it were cold
> And in the icy silence of the tomb,
> So haunt thy days and chill thy dreaming nights
> That thou wouldst wish thine own heart dry of blood
> So in my veins red life might stream again,
> And thou be conscience-calm'd—See here it is—
> I hold it towards you.
>
> (1819)

The first thing to note is that as a dramatic lyric it begins by powerfully presenting a thing in the world: this living hand. It then unfolds its anguished argument in a series of rhetorical clauses and elegantly balanced phrases that are designed to seduce through guilt and confuse with their quick shifts back and forth across the threshold between living and dead: I'm alive, but if I were dead, you'd wish you were dead, so that I could be alive again and you wouldn't feel guilty. "Guilty about what?" the befuddled and anxious object of this strange address might ask, and then the poem makes its move— Never mind that, remember my hand? See, here it is, I hold it toward you.

With what extraordinary power and presentational magic those last nine words appear out of the (intentional) thicket of rhetoric. It's as if the page rips apart and an actual hand reaches toward the reader in a gesture that fuses pleading and seduction tinged with subliminal menace. Not only is "Lines Supposed to Have Been Addressed to Fanny Brawne" an excellent example of implied gesture and idiomatic speech, it is also a powerful example of the dramatic lyric as an interaction of self and other. The lyric anguish of the self, its irrational protest against the conditions of being, is no longer directed upward toward some transcendent goal outside time—no bright star, steadfast and unchangeable, no "immortal" bird. It is self to other self, and both are permeated with the conditions of being—riddled with time and mortality; both are swept along on the dark flood. Against this deathward-sweeping rhetorical flow the poem proposes the rescuing gesture of clasped hands, of bodies clinging in passionate union even as they drown, their utmost possibilities ("earnest grasping" and "warmth") not solutions but at most consolations.

From Lyric to Dramatic Lyric: The Case of Yeats

The very self-enclosing qualities of the lyric that tortured Keats reassured young Yeats. Moody, melancholy, shy—Yeats had little of the emotional volatility Keats exhibited and that made the earliest of Keats's lyrics an agonized thrashing, a "fever of [the] self." For the youthful Yeats, poetry functioned in large part as a defense, as did his occult studies, against his father's materialism and that of the surrounding Victorian culture. He was from the start powerfully attracted to fin de siècle notions of the cult of art and the cult of the artist, whether embodied by Oscar Wilde and Walter Pater, or by Mallarmé (a number of whose Tuesday soirées he attended in Paris).

Though in his essay "The Philosophy of Shelley's Poetry" (1900) Yeats shows himself to be aware of the "self-entrancing" dangers of the "subjective lyric," most of his early writing is deeply preoccupied with lyric ideals and absolutes. In that same essay, he discusses "symbol" as a main avenue to the transcendent lyric state: "he [Shelley] could hardly have helped perceiving that an image that has transcended particular time and place becomes a symbol, passes beyond death, as it were, and becomes a living soul."

This bias against the world of contingency, the timebound world of particulars, will persist throughout Yeats's life—it is the mark of the lyric temperament. But only the young Yeats would be so absolute as to want his brand of symbolism to return and "cast out descriptions of nature for the sake of nature, of the moral law for the sake of the moral law, a casting out of all anecdotes and of that brooding over scientific opinion that so often extinguished the central flame in Tennyson" ("The Symbolism of Poetry," 1900).

For the young Yeats, contact with the lyric world doesn't result in an annihilation of self, a Keatsean wish to "fade away into the forest dim." Yeats's lyric persona is the magician who calls power down from the unconditional world into the self: "I cannot now think symbols less than the greatest of all powers whether they are used consciously by the masters of magic, or half unconsciously by their successors, the poet, the musician and the artist" ("Magic," 1901).

His early lyric self is an aggrandizement of solitariness. He is not "forlorn" as Keats is, but presents himself as the proud man apart, one of those "lean and fierce minds who are at war with their times." He seeks no imaginative flight toward the nightingale, but would instead, through the (literal) magic of symbol, "call down" into the poet's self the transcendent world of "divine order, divine beauty": "Whatever the passions of men have gathered about, becomes a symbol in the Great Memory, and in the hands of him who has the secret it is a worker of wonders, a caller-up of angels or of devils."

Though the main function of the symbol as thus defined is to allow the solitary self to make contact with beings and powers arrayed at the apex and nadir of the vertical lyric hierarchy (angels and devils), another aspect of the symbol allows it to function effectively on the horizontal plane where self encounters other selves. Much of Yeats's essay on magic recounts those experiments with fellow adepts in which he would concentrate on visualizing a symbol and that same or a related image would appear spontaneously in the other person's mind. Such "proof" of the symbol's power to connect one person to another, albeit occultly, was all that the young Yeats needed or wanted of connection to the horizontal, conditional world.

Not only symbol but a certain peculiar approach to rhythm was integral to creating his version of the pure lyric as spiritual cocoon:

> The purpose of rhythm, it has always seemed to me, is to prolong the moment of contemplation, the moment when we are both asleep and awake, which is the one moment of creation, by hushing us with an alluring monotony, while it holds us waking by variety, to keep us in that state of perhaps real trance, in which the mind liberated from the pressure of the will is unfolded by symbols. ("The Symbolism of Poetry")

To completely achieve the insular lyric he aspired to in his first books, Yeats combined his lulling, trance-inducing rhythms and theory of the lyric symbol with a third essential element: the absence of an other, whose reality (as noun in the poem, as resistance to the "I" in the dramatic setting of the poem) would bring the self into a dialectic relationship with the conditional world. Here is "He Reproves the Curlew," a poem from his third collection, *The Wind Among the Reeds*, published when he was thirty-four:

> O curlew, cry no more in the air,
> Or only to the water in the West;
> Because your crying brings to my mind
> Passion-dimmed eyes and long heavy hair
> That was shaken out over my breast:
> There is enough evil in the crying of wind.

The lulling rhythm he seeks is accomplished by the dominant anapests and accented, for passion's sake, with the adjectival stress clusters of the fourth line. Though Yeats's early lyrics of melancholy loneliness characteristically make reference to an other, a beloved, this other is frequently (as in this poem) safely out of the picture, out of the story—disembodied and assimilated into idealizing memory. Seldom is a real other present to give the poem's self some resistance and thus generate the necessary tensions and dichotomies of story. Even the curlew—which might be thought to have bird-substance, bird-otherness—is only present as "crying," as sound.

Or take another poem from the same collection, "A Poet to His Beloved":

> I bring you with reverent hands
> The books of my numberless dreams,
> White woman that passion has worn
> As the tide wears the dove-gray sand,
> And with heart more old than the horn
> That is brimmed from the pale fire of time:
> White woman with numberless dreams,
> I bring you my passionate rhyme.

Here the incantatory intent of the rhythm is even more pronounced. We can try to be fooled into thinking there is an actual narrative going on here ("I bring you . . . books . . ."), but the constant interrupton of the narrative by evocative images and the final circularity and repetitiveness demonstrated by the last two lines show that this is not an event in the world, but an excuse for a kind of morbid self-excitement on the poet's part that is taking place in the adjectives, that most passive part of speech: "reverent," "numberless," "white," "dove-gray," "pale," "white," "numberless," "passionate." One suspects that this poet will swoon long before he delivers the package of poems to the lady in question.

When we move on to the opening stanza of "The Wild Swans at Coole" (published in 1916), we are immediately aware of the presence of the natural world as an entity in its own right, the conditional world undistorted by excessive subjectivity. The adjectives are not incantatory and vaguely evocative but are doing their job of making the objects more precise: "autumn," "woodland," "October," "still," "brimming," "nine-and-fifty." The entire first stanza consists of a presentation of a scene in the world, a landscape outside the self:

> The trees are in their autumn beauty,
> The woodland paths are dry,
> Under the October twilight the water
> Mirrors a still sky;
> Upon the brimming water among the stones
> Are nine-and-fifty swans.

The self doesn't even enter the poem until the opening of the second stanza, and then only as a reflective consciousness offering more objective factual background (nineteen years ago I was here first), and also asserting the self as an actor in the landscape (a counter of swans). It is only in the third stanza that the lyric self asserts its presence and still (importantly) in response to an event in the world ("I have looked upon those brilliant creatures, and now my heart is sore"). It may be the same old melancholy Yeats of the earlier poems (who is to say the self's temperament can change?), but the melancholy is not a watercolor wash over the whole scene; it is presented as a product of the interaction of self and world: a dialectic of melancholy in which the reader can evaluate (among other things) whether the emotion and the event that occasioned it have any explicable and convincing correlation.

During the seventeen years between publication of *The Wind Among the Reeds* and *The Wild Swans at Coole,* Yeats was far more involved in worldly affairs. Specifically, he had spent ten years working to found an Irish nationalist theater, writing plays himself and setting up and running the Abbey Theatre in Dublin. Such activity meant much less time devoted to poetry; he himself claimed not to have written a lyric for the space of five years. But it also meant a heightened awareness of the elements of drama, a shift from contemplation toward action.

Still (and always) a symbolist, Yeats was in the process of shifting his loyalties from one kind of symbol to another. He had himself distinguished two kinds of symbols, the intellectual symbol and the emotional symbol, in his early essay, "The Symbolism of Poetry." Emotional symbols "evoke emotion alone," whereas intellectual symbols "evoke ideas alone, or ideas mingled with emotions." Shakespeare was only interested in emotional symbols "that he may come nearer to our sympathy," with the final result that "one is mixed with the whole spectacle of the world"; whereas Dante or the myth of Demeter concerned only intellectual symbols whereby "one is mixed with the shadow of God or of a goddess" until one moves "among divine people, and things that have shaken off our mortality." Needless to say, the early Yeats of *The Wind*

Among the Reeds professed total loyalty to the lyric pretensions of the intellectual symbol, which promised to elevate poet and audience alike to the realm of the gods. But by the time of *The Wild Swans at Coole* and his later work, it is fair to say that Yeats's involvement with theater made the emotional symbol far more attractive to him. The emotional symbol's intensities, its powers of attraction and repulsion, which were themselves dramatic actions and movement—all these qualities become more powerfully present in his later work.

The shift in emphasis to the emotional symbol represents an opening to the disorder of the conditional world. In another early discussion of symbols, Yeats intuited the limits of his own too-ordered lyrics and saw a solution in the multivalent aspect of "ancient" symbols:

> It is only by ancient symbols, by symbols that have numberless meanings besides the one or two the writer lays emphasis upon, or the half-score he knows of, that any highly subjective art can escape from the barrenness and shallowness of a too conscious arrangement, into the abundance and depth of Nature. ("The Philosophy of Shelley's Poetry")

Surely the poem "Easter 1916" is a watershed in Yeats's work. In it the conditional world intrudes upon the self in the violent and typically Irish form of politics and history. No poet in Ireland from the seventeenth century on has ever entirely escaped issues of history and politics, but for Yeats "Easter 1916" represents a new level of self-in-the-world. By this time (the poem was published in 1921), Yeats had been deeply involved in politics and literary politics and theater for years.

The initial persona of this poem is not the self-absorbed lyric self of his melancholic youth but a different form of self-enclosure: a smug man-of-the-world. It is another form of the self that will not have its affairs or feelings intruded upon, that will not be affected by realities outside its control:

> I have met them at close of day
> Coming with vivid faces
> From counter or desk among grey
> Eighteenth-century houses.

> I have passed with a nod of the head
> Or polite meaningless words,
> Or have lingered awhile and said
> Polite meaningless words,
> And thought before I had done
> Of a mocking tale or a gibe
> To please a companion
> Around the fire at the club,
> Being certain that they and I
> But lived where motley is worn.

Yeats is setting up a persona to be knocked down, jolted out of its complacency, by an event in the world. The self is jolted out of the timeless, lyric time of theater (we "but lived where motley is worn"—that is, as clowns on a stage) into the world's time: the flow of event, of action, reaction, and consequence. (This stanza also accomplishes a rare event: Yeats overcomes, for this moment, his disdain for the Irish middle class).

Stanza 2 gives us Yeats's undeceived assessments of the mundane lives and characters of four of the leaders of the Easter Rising, only to conclude that each has been "changed, changed utterly" by his or her heroic deeds.

We have already seen that symbol is the main avenue by which the poet/magus makes contact with the lyric unconditional, and is thus a fundamental ordering principle in Yeats's work. The transformation undergone by the four leaders demonstrates another way in which mortals transcend the conditional world they inhabit, one I will call "heroic identification." Heroic identification becomes Yeats's second major ordering principle, a sort of narrative variant of symbol and one especially useful for making sense of the chaos of history and politics. We see it when the rebels transcend their limits, resign their parts in the "casual comedy" to take on heroic or tragic roles (as with Lear, Timon, and Cordelia in "Lapis Lazuli"—who are "worthy their prominent part in the play"). We see it when Yeats consistently casts Maud Gonne as Helen of Troy. We see it in Yeats himself, when, as an old man in "An Acre of Grass," he declares:

> Myself must I remake
> Till I am Timon and Lear
> Or that William Blake
> Who beat upon the wall
> Till truth obeyed his call.

In heroic identification, in contrast to the symbol, it is the human figure that is transformed, not just an object in the world. Likewise, through action and deed the transfigured hero or heroine extends his or her symbolic power into drama. It is as if a little patch of the horizontal, conditional world (that inhabited by the "transfigured" person) were lifted up into the lyric world, or at the very least were lifted up to hover above the earth, where all with eyes could gaze with awe at the spectacle. Though in some sense this is no more than a variant of the idealization of the hero or heroine, it is for Yeats a fundamental way of reconciling his lyric longings with the conditional world. These figures move in the world, but they are not, in the right circumstances, "of the world."

To return to "Easter 1916," stanza 3 presents the origins and preconditions of the rebels' transformation—singleness of purpose is shown to have magical power:

> Hearts with one purpose alone
> Through summer and winter seem
> Enchanted to a stone.

The stanza continues as a marvelous "digression" in which the chaos of the conditional world whirls around the heart/stone that has been transformed by contact with an absolute ideal.

Stanza 4 continues the stone image briefly, only long enough to level an essential charge against lyric transformation: it is bought at the price of all human sympathy:

> Too long a sacrifice
> Can make a stone of the heart.

Later in stanza 4, the poem struggles against the self's impulse to tame the chaotic, historical event with an incantatory rhetorical digression that culminates in a euphemistic metaphor:

>   our part
> To murmur name upon name,
> As a mother names her child
> When sleep at last has come
> On limbs that had run wild.
> What is it but nightfall?
> No, no, not night but death.

Such a metaphor, if accepted, would be a way of taking the event back inside the poet's imagination and away from its place of origin as a fact in the world, and it must be repudiated.

Though the speaker castigates himself in the poem for his recurring attempts to evade reality and return to a smug, self-enclosed consciousness, he is not denigrating the self and asserting the necessary primacy of the world. The complex dialectic of self and world in "Easter 1916" has expanded beyond simply the speaker and the world to include autonomous, named others, but if we fail to see that these others are carrying the moral perspective of the lyric self we have missed an important point. Their excessive dream, that is, their lyric longing for an absolute and unconditional reality, has caused this important event in the world. The martyrs may have been "bewildered" dreamers (so like lyric poets), but their very intensity and its consequences have permanently altered reality:

> We know their dream; enough
> To know they dreamed and are dead;
> And what if excess of love
> Bewildered them till they died?
> I write it out in verse—
> MacDonagh and MacBride
> And Connoly and Pearse
> Now and in time to be,
> Wherever green is worn,
> Are changed, changed utterly:
> A terrible beauty is born.

The term that dominates the refrain, and the entire poem, is itself a reconciliation of the conditional and the lyric: "terrible beauty." A beauty that has opened itself to the violence and chaos of the historical, conditional world, the world of terror. How far we are from his earlier lyric allegiance to "divine beauty, divine order."

Yeats himself was aware that the events of 1916 were pivotal in his work: "Sometimes I am told in commendation, if the newspaper is Irish, in condemnation if English, that my movement perished under the firing squads of 1916; sometimes that those firing squads made our realistic movement possible" ("A General Introduction to My Work," 1937).

In the same essay, he zeroes in on the same historical moment to locate a formal transformation of his work: "It was a long time before I had made a language to my liking; I began to make it when I discovered some twenty years ago [that is, around 1917] that I must seek . . . a powerful and passionate syntax, and a complete coincidence between period and stanza." In other words, not only has Yeats opened himself to the thematic disorder of history and politics, but his attitude toward rhythm has shifted drastically toward a vitalizing disorder as he weds "passionate syntax" to "passionate subject matter." As his essay makes clear, this is not a leap into chaos—he counterbalances his formal disorder of syntax with a system of stanza form and with "traditional meters," and his thematic disorder is ordered by symbols and heroic identification. But he now has in place all the necessary terms and tools for a fundamentally dialectical relationship between his lyric longing and the conditional world.

Why not go one step further and have the self as an active participant in the world: out there moving through the truth of the world (the schoolroom) gathering facts and yet always on the verge of becoming absorbed by the truth of the lyric self as well (in the forms of idealizing memory and imagination). I'm thinking here, of course, of Yeats's "Among School Children," which appeared in 1928, a poem supremely fluid in its movements in and out of the two realities:

> I walk through the long schoolroom questioning;
> A kind old nun in a white hood replies;
> The children learn to cipher and to sing,

> To study reading-books and history,
> To cut and sew, be neat in everything
> In the best modern way—the children's eyes
> In momentary wonder stare upon
> A sixty-year-old smiling public man.
>
> I dream of a Ledaean body, bent
> Above a sinking fire, a tale that she
> Told of a harsh reproof, or trivial event
> That changed some childish day to tragedy—
> Told, and it seemed our two natures blent
> Into a sphere from youthful sympathy,
> Or else, to alter Plato's parable,
> Into the yolk and white of the one shell.

And so on . . .

Here action and reaction, a series of dialectical exchanges, go back and forth as the speaker's emotional state intensifies. In addition to numerous other issues, Yeats works in "Among School Children" to reconcile the symbolic and heroic with the mortal and mundane—to see the mortal child in the demi-goddess and vice versa:

> And wonder if she looked so at that age—
> For even daughters of the swan can share
> Something of every paddler's heritage—
> And had that colour upon cheek or hair,
> And thereupon my heart is driven wild:
> She stands before me as a living child.

By section 6, the poem is ready to note a series of historical visions on the nature of reality (Plato's, Aristotle's, Pythagoras'), only to lump them together in a dismissive image:

> Old clothes upon old sticks to scare a bird

an image that picks up his earlier image of his own bodily decrepitude ("a comfortable kind of old scarecrow") and anticipates by contrast the dynamic image that resolves the entire poem. Section 7 raises the possibility that it is better to be loyal to transcendent symbols that "keep a marble or a bronze repose" than to worship the time-trapped images of real children, but concludes that both mortals and symbols "break hearts." In other words, the tragic disorder of suffering is inescapable. How can such a situation be convincingly ordered and resolved? By a symbol that incarnates and reconciles both longings, both realites of being and becoming, the transcendent and the conditional. Resolving it also in the form of a question—that is, by an acknowledgment of the limits of our ability to assert. (If he were to sum up all his message in a single sentence, the elderly Yeats wrote, it would be "man can embody the truth, but he cannot know it"—itself a reconciling of the two truths, an incarnating and dramatizing statement.) Most of all, resolve by a vision, but not a static one:

> O body swayed to music, O brightening glance,
> How can we know the dancer from the dance?

No one familiar with Yeats's work and temperament would claim that Yeats was ever reconciled to the conditional world—to him it was, to the very end, a squalid "rag and bone shop," and he far preferred symbols, those "masterful images" that were complete and "grew in pure mind." But he was a genius at presenting the tension between lyric longing and the power of the conditional world, and a number of his greatest poems are dramatic lyrics moving nimbly up and down the ladders that connect these two worlds.

A Cluster of Quotations and Notes

On the Lyric

The lyric premise—irrational premise—is that an individual poem can become the (temporary) center of a solar system, constellating around it certain planets (called words) and the rest darkness and silence. This absurd premise is necessary in order for the lyric to bring us its truth, to body forth its truth.

* * *

The subjective (lyric) poet being contrasted with the "objective poet" who concerns himself with external things and actions: "He [the subjective poet] . . . is impelled to embody the thing he perceives, not so much with reference to the many below as to the one above him, the supreme Intelligence which apprehends all things in their absolute truth,—an ultimate view ever aspired to, if but partially attained, by the poet's own soul. Not what man sees, but what God sees—the Ideas of Plato, seeds of creation lying burningly on the Divine Hand—it is toward these that he struggles. Not with the combination of humanity in action but with the primal elements of humanity he has to do; and he digs where he stands—preferring to seek them in his own soul as the nearest reflex of that absolute Mind, according to the intuitions of which he desires to perceive and speak. Such a poet does not deal habitually with the picturesque groupings and tempestuous tossings of the forest-trees, but

---

Previously unpublished.

with their roots and fibres naked to the chalk and stone" (Browning, "Shelley and the Art of Poetry," 1851).

* * *

There is, in the personal lyric that interests me, a longing for the unconditional, a longing to transcend the conditions of being (time, space). We see it in Keats's *Endymion*—"Wherein lies happiness? In . . . fellowship divine, / A fellowship with essence; till we shine / Full-alchemiz'd and free of space."

Or ran across it the other day in James Wright's translation of Hesse's poem "The Poet": "the one who looks on, the bearer of human longing."

And what social task can be accomplished by someone as alienated as this lyric poet? Such a poet is "the voice of the solitary / Who makes others less alone" (Stanley Kunitz, "Revolving Meditation").

* * *

Lyric longing insists on absolutes, on unities. As such, lyric longing is at war with the world—the world is becoming, change, multiplicity. The world is the Many, the lyric desires the One.

Jarrell's "The Old and the New Masters" as a lyric retort to Auden's "Musée des Beaux Arts" about suffering, about adoration. Jarrell claims that everything/everyone crystallizes around the lyric moment of intensity. The "new masters" (Auden) put "the crucifixion / In one corner of the canvas." Moved from the center (lyric position) to the periphery, a decentering tied to science. Finally, the transition is complete. What began in the lyric:

> everything
> That was or will be in the world is fixed
> On its small, helpless, human center.
> (*The Lost World*, p. 65)

ends with:

> in the corner
> Is the small radioactive planet men called Earth.

According to this poem, lyric art places a thing (of worship) at the center; science disperses from the center. Art that follows science ("the new way") betrays the issues of suffering and worship (adoration), which only the lyric attitude can give meaning to, can make moral by making central, by bringing into lyric focus.

* * *

"A longing grows to return to the open composition in which the accidents and imperfections of speech might awake intimations of human being. He searches for quality like a jeweler—and he is dependent one suspects on whether his emotion (which he polishes) is a diamond or not. That is, he would attempt to cut any stone diamond-wise, to force his emotion to the test. He would discover much if he also would cut paper-crowns or scatter the pebbles and litter of a mind wherever he goes" (Robert Duncan, "On Quality and Poems," from Donald Allen's *New American Poetry*). The above a caution to the lyric poet—the constellator and diamond-cutter in myself.

* * *

Rilke's vision of Paris as a city of hospitals and the sick, sickness, and ugliness everywhere—a vision made vivid in *Notebooks of Malte Laurids Brigge*. Mallarmé saying "To say 'I am happy' is to say 'I am a coward' and more often 'I am a fool': for either one must fail to see the sky of the Ideal and the ceiling of happiness, or one must deliberately close one's eyes. I have made a little poem of these ideas: Les Fenêtres." The image of hospitals and illness (Keats's "here where we sit and hear each other groan"; Baudelaire's cry—"Anywhere out of this world!"). You don't see the pathological repulsion at this world in Rilke's poems (there it is more likely to be a positive lyric longing), but in his *Notebooks* you have the underbelly of the lyric spirit.

Eliot is a major example of this pathology. He's less attracted by a positive vision (a "bright star") than he is repulsed by the conditional world. The bodily, the sexual and sensual—his motivation tends to be uncontrollable guilt, fear, and disgust at these things rather than an attraction to the spiritual (or that's what his first book proclaims to me). The resolution of his attraction/repulsion ends in favor of repulsion. The stasis of "teach us to be still" rather than the animation of desire. The girl of "La Figlia che Piange" who is implored to "stand on the highest pavement of the stair" and not to move, not to descend. Movement (born of desire) is fatal—"Till human voices wakes us, and we drown"—drown in the conditional.

* * *

"Nothing leads more certainly to perfect barbarity than an exclusive attachment to the pure spirit.... I have been intimately acquainted with this fanaticism." (Paul Valéry, 1926, quoted in Edgar Wind's *Art and Anarchy*)

* * *

System-making (ideology) is the death of the individual, the death of the spontaneous and various response to experience (which lyric poetry represents). As such, it is the death of poetry.

Vision emerges; it does not descend, nor is it imposed from without. It emerges from the self (or else it will exclude and oppress the self).

Lyric vision is one of the social tasks of the poet in modern times (see Akhmatova, "Poem without a Hero").

From the self outward—through the self outward. But first self, and self with some innerness, some consciousness—not just an actor, but also an actor (an interacter with the world).

* * *

"Only he understands what the (lyric) poem says who perceives in its solitude the voice of humanity; indeed the loneliness of the lyric expression itself is latent in our individualistic and, ultimately, atomistic society—just as, by contrast, its general binding validity derives from the denseness of its individuation." (Adorno, "Lyric Poetry and Society")

* * *

Because the lyric temperament is obsessive (it's wellspring and limit), it is likely to project itself out onto a single object, rather than, say, a variety of objects in a single poem. That variety of objects represents either the mental freedom or the illusion of mental freedom characteristic of a meditative poem. The latter is a poem that "feels free to" consider various thoughts or things.

I don't think the lyric temperament, by its very nature, has imaginative freedom. Its external limiting conditions (time, space) are mirrored by internal limiting conditions (obsessions) that it also yearns to transcend. In its anguish, it is at odds with the inner world as well as the outer world.

* * *

Found myself (at 4 A.M.) wondering about what I'm calling healing modes of imagination in poetry, in the dramatic lyric (namely sympathy, eros, symbol in the Post-confessional essay). I've already asserted that these are forms that lyric longing takes. They are clearly means of transcending the self and its circumstances. I found myself thinking this morning about those things Viktor Frankl found had survival value in the concentration camps: love (dialogue with and meditations on the absent beloved), beauty in nature, and humor. Aren't they all modes of transcendence? Is healing related to survival? Elizabeth Bishop, who insisted on art as healing in an exchange with Lowell, was never healed really, but she did survive.

Most of the Post-confessionals did—and isn't that my point? The survival value of these lyric modes, of modes of transcendence that we see constantly modeled for us in poems—Whitman and Dickinson, Keats and Bishop and Rich: one of the things they are doing is modeling modes of survival; how the self survives the miseries it finds itself among—its own personal miseries and also "the giant agony of the world" (Keats's phrase from "The Fall of Hyperion").

On Dramatic Lyric

The personal lyric (glimpsed first in English with Wyatt's "They Flee from Me")—its achievement is to inject individual personality into the lyric. To create personality through the distinctive use of speech rhythms (I call it "urgent speech"). It's there full-blown a little later in Herbert's "The Collar" and "Love (ii)."

* * *

Aspects of the dramatic lyric:

1. Injecting personality into the lyric through urgent speech.
2. "Gestural speech" as expressed by Brecht (his example from the Gospels, "if thine eye offend thee, pluck it out," seems to emphasize the dramatic, gestural possibilities of syntax and phrasing/pauses. Good example of both: Herbert's "The Collar").
3. The existence of an other—a resistance to the self, something against which the self (the "I" of the poem) can struggle and define itself. This other creates the conflict necessary for story to exist.

* * *

Worringer, in his *Abstraction and Empathy* (1911), wants art to abandon the human figure and its agony, wants transcendence with a vengeance—the sort of transcendence that I consider the pathological aspect of the lyric spirit, that longing for "purity" which is antilife.

I understand Worringer's transcendental urge—his terror at the world (for example, "Poem in October" in my first book; or the Stone poems, where the Wound appears and he knows it will be different: "now there will be footprints"). But I also know that the sexual exchange is something I feel a powerful need to celebrate (how placing the sexual exchange at the center of meaning calls for "human grace" as a model for art and also for involvement with the conditional world, since that is where the desired Other is). It is "the flowery band that binds us to the earth."

So, to me, I feel the terror (the thanatos principle—that which wants to draw back, withdraw, isolate itself and disidentify) and I also feel the eros impulse—to touch, to connect, to identify with the other. The two together are what I know: lyric longing and longing for the world. Again, I propose the dramatic lyric as the appropriate form for the interplay of these forces: it tells us about the innerness of the self and it tell us about the impinging reality of the other in the conditional world.

* * *

I've always wanted the spirit to descend and incarnate—as in "We Must Make a Kingdom of It" where it "bends down from its tall stalk"—but I've also felt the urge for wings.

* * *

The need for a moral dimension in poems—how that can happen when a self and an other are present. The moral tension in addition to dramatic tension in the dramatic lyric. Roethke's exploration of love, power, and fear in "My Papa's Waltz" and then in the late poem "The Meadow Mouse" (where the perspective and proportions are reversed: in the former, the I was small and vulnerable, the other huge; in the later poem, the I is huge, the other cowers). Or Robert Hayden's "Those Winter Sundays." How a primary relationship is essential as a structure. E.g., how Herbert's "The Collar" resolves its tension in father/child relationship. This primary relationship makes it possible to explore or dramatize moral issues (love, power) as well as existential issues. Keats's "Ode to a Nightingale" is an existential drama, his "Lines Supposed to Have Been Addressed to Fanny Brawne" is a moral drama as well—not in the sense of right and wrong, but in the sense of dramatized, concretized ambivalence: the full expression of the ambivalent nature of human dilemmas.

* * *

Existential dramas: self and mysteries of consciousness; example: Keats's "Ode to a Nightingale."

* * *

"Moral" dramas: self and other (a primary relationship): love and power; example: Keats's "Lines Supposed to Have Been Addressed to Fanny Brawne."

* * *

One thing I'm exploring in my effort to diffentiate dramatic lyric from lyric: that the extension of the lyric in the direction of action/narrative is a step toward the creation of a personality, because, as Aristotle points out, deeds define character. The extension of the lyric toward action is one way personality/persona may be created.

* * *

Keats's decision to drop the original first stanza of "Ode on Melancholy" is the lyric "carver's" decision (to cut away toward the pure form, the essence).

But it's also the dramatist's in that the poem now begins with emphatic gestic language:

> No, no! Go not to Lethe, neither twist
>   Wolf's-bane, tight-rooted, for its poisonous wine

instead of:

> Though you should build a bark of dead men's bones
>   And rear a platform gibbet for a mast

The original is both pictorial and passive.

* * *

Reading Michael Ryan's "Poetry and the Audience" and Louis Simpson's "The Character of the Poet":

William Carlos Williams (quoted by Simpson): "The first thing that stands eternally in the way of really good writing is always one: the virtual impossibility of lifting to the imagination those things which lie under the direct scrutiny of the senses."

Simpson: "How can we lift to the imagination those things which lie under the direct scrutiny of the senses? By lifting ourselves—there is no other way. We know what the poet does—she absorbs what she sees and transforms it. Whitman has described the process of absorbing:

> There was a boy went forth every day
> And the first object he look'd upon, that object he became

Simpson laments the lack of imagination in American poetry—without imagination no transfiguration, no "lifting up" as Williams calls for. Simpson sees this as the trivial dead end of confessional writing. Later, he begins his attack on the lyric: that the decline in general interest in poetry is related to the rise of the lyric and "it is the nature of the lyric to express a subjective mood and ignore the outer reality."

(I have my share of agreement with him—that's why I speak of the dramatic lyric: self in the world yet aware of lyric longing. The talk on Keats and Yeats moving from lyric to dramatic lyric.)

Both Simpson and Ryan want a return to narrative. The idea of narrative as being outside the self and as being more shareable, less narcissistic. My interest is in story which is not really narrative. And also, finally, we are seeing here an intelligent *War against the lyric*. But what Simpson means by the lyric is the "pure lyric" of Mallarmé and Stevens, that lineage. Simpson's program (which corresponds to his own work, which shouldn't be surprising): "The city is antipoetic, the suburbs are antipoetic, but turn to the people, and subjects for poetry abound. This is the solution to our present difficulty, the emptiness and unimportance of American verse. We need a poetry of human situations. Imagination does not consist of thinking of surrealist imagery."

Thinking about the Ryan and Simpson essays read yesterday. What they have in common: a belief in narrative, in connecting to the rest of the human community, a left politics, a hostility to the genteel poetry now dominant, a sense of Whitman and Wordsworth as conceptual forebears, simplicity as a virtue in writing. Where they differ: Simpson thinks free verse is necessary and formal verse inadvertently reactionary; Ryan feels sustained by linking his argument to the "classical" and "tribal" by way of Gilbert Murray.

Where I fit in. Mostly agree where they agree. Differ at that point where, say, Baudelaire matters to me, but not to either of them so far as I know. What do I mean by "Baudelaire"? A self dramatizing its conflicting intensities. A self tortured by sin, delighted by sensuality and vice, tortured by and attracted to the ideal. And what is the ideal?

I don't quite know. Simpson dislikes the lyric—I love story, but I also love a metaphysical story/lyric of the sort I try to do in "Song of the Invisible Corpse," "We Must Make a Kingdom of It," or "The Tree"—some sense of wanting to get the pure, passionate essence of the self the way Sappho does. She's always Sappho, but I don't feel at all excluded from her lyrics.

The ideal I seek in the metaphysical lyrics wouldn't be a transcendent thing in a Mallarméan "purity" sense—it would be simply a belief that a few words, images, and gestures could surround a sufficient mystery.

That's one of my lyric ambitions: to surround, with a few words, images, gestures and a minimal story structure, a sufficient mystery. How do you know you've succeeded? You feel it—like holding a small bird in your hands, you feel the intense life struggling to get out yet held there.

* * *

I also have a real interest in the complex narratives that Ryan and Simpson write and espouse. I want to write them also, am trying to in "On a Highway East of Selma, Alabama," "Hotel St. Louis," "The Post Office," and others. But I want both. I want to be able to write the narratives in verse paragraphs and the metaphysical lyrics. And something in between like "The Cherry Orchards." But above all, intensity.

On Symbol

Paraphrase from Suzanne Langer's *Mind: An Essay on Human Feeling* (vol. 3, pp. 45–50): How the human mind is differentiated from the animal mind by its ability to *project* the self into objects. This begins somatically: our sense of balance (of "static mechanics") is visually projected into an object such that the object is seen as having the quality of being "stable" or "off-balance." Chimpanzees (observed by Kohler) can't do that (example of ladder and suspended bananas; chimps won't angle the ladder against the wall; only see ladder as tool, not as stable/unstable, not themselves as other).

From this objectification of our subjective sense (balance)

we receive back (or so it seems) this subjective sense of the object: we project out in order to receive back (great survival ability). Thus the object becomes an elementary symbol (in this instance containing almost no ideation).

From here to more sophisticated projections of internal states isn't far. The ability (inevitability) to project is the essential thing.

* * *

"The soul or spirit transmits itself into all matter—into rocks, and can live the life of a rock—into the sea, and can feel itself the sea—into the oak or other tree—into an animal, and feel itself a horse, a fish, or bird—into the earth—into the motions of the suns and stars—

"A man is only interested in anything when he identifies himself with it—he must himself be whirling and speeding through space like the planet Mercury—he must be driving like a cloud—he must shine like the sun—he must be orbic and balanced in the air, like this earth—he must crawl like the pismire—he must—he would be growing fragrantly in the air, like the locust blossoms—he would rumble and crash like the thunder in the sky—he would spring like a cat on his prey—he would splash like a whale." (Whitman, quoted by Paul Zweig, *Walt Whitman: The Making of the Poet*, p. 174)

* * *

Projection is the primary act of the human mind (see Langer), and this projection is called "imagination" in poetry. These images are "emanations of felt truth" as Stanley Kunitz puts it. In the same passage, Kunitz remarks that the human mind, in the act of dreaming, manifests several ways of thought that also characterize the waking poet's mind, namely: substitution, displacement, and fusion (that is, Freud's dream processes). These are clearly acts of intelligence—associative, nonrational intelligence that spontaneously manifests itself in images.

* * *

Stanley Kunitz's concept of the "key image" is central to understanding lyric (subjective symbolizing) consciousness. "That cluster of key images is the purest concentration of self, the individuating node, the place where the persona starts. When fresh thoughts and sensations enter the mind, some of them are drawn into the gravitational field of the old life and cohere to it. Out of these combining elements, the more resistant the better, poetry happens" ("From Feathers to Iron").

Kunitz's notion of the key image as inexhaustible and extensive (over the life's work) as well as intensive in its meanings is crucial. The recurring pattern of key images gives us access to the themes and meanings of a poet of subjective imagination.

* * *

Symbol is an object that has received a subjective projection. The most effective literary symbols are those which constitute a dynamic reconciliation of opposites (the "bittersweet" of Sappho, or the Taoist yin-yang). This sort of symbol is one of the primary human resources for registering our conceptual awareness of the simultaneity of contrary feelings, contrary truths. As with the yin-yang figure conceived as fluid, there will always be a predominantly positive or negative coloring to a symbol, but always its opposite will be present also, however modestly. Likewise, a given symbol will concretize a dominant idea or emotion, but may also concretize its opposite in a modest way as well.

* * *

"This coincidence of opposite processes and notions (such as birth and death) in a single representation characterizes the peculiar unity of the liminal: that which is neither this nor that, and yet both."

"Sacra"—sacred articles revealed during initiations. "A striking feature of such sacred articles is their formal simplicity. It is their interpretation which is complex, not their outward form." (Victor Turner?)

* * *

"The symbol gives rise to thought." (Paul Ricoeur)

* * *

"In certain almost supernatural states of soul/mind, the profundity of life reveals itself entirely in the spectacle that is before your eyes, no matter how ordinary it is. It becomes symbol." (Baudelaire, from *Fusées*. Congruent with Wordsworth's "spots of time.")

* * *

What I hate is the notion that symbols have to indicate Symbolism and Mallarméan "evocation" and pure transcendence. I prefer to think of them as that place where two worlds intersect—the one of the embedded flow of the poem's narrative world; the other, the vertical story indicated by the transcendent element in the symbol.

* * *

Sometimes metaphor is horizontal symbol, symbol where the two elements, the narrative object and the lyric meaning, are made explicit and placed side by side, as in my own "flotsam of cow bones in a plowed field" where death is a shipwreck and the furrowed earth is the sea, with all its implications that to be alive, to walk the earth is a dangerous miracle. Not all metaphors are of this type (some might be merely descriptive, as when Bishop says the dogwood blossoms have a cigarette burn at the end of each petal).

* * *

The propaganda of the Imagists was essential, but they didn't abide by it: how quickly Pound's "intellectual and emotional complex in an instant of time" (an excellent definition of symbol) was abandoned for the "radiant node or cluster" of Vorticism, which explicitly rejected psychology and thus moved away from its ability to pay attention to the "dark passages" of consciousness.

* * *

Edgar Wind on the triad of the Graces as "unfolded Venus." That this is how Unity manifests its multiplicity—its contradictory nature is shown in the two extremes and the third term that mediates between the two extremes. Like my description of poem as "story": the two contraries and the resolution in terms of a third thing that reconciles the contraries (and symbolically embodies them) thus releasing the tension of the story; e.g., father and son in Hayden's "Those Winter Sundays" are "reconciled" by the shoes. Or the milder tensions of self and world, self and others in Bishop's "Santarém" are reconciled in the wasp's nest the pharmacist gives her (only to be undercut by Mr. Swan's final, nihilistic remark at poem's end).

On Eros and the Body

That there is, before and beneath all the ambiguity, impossibility, or absurdity of language, a human impulse of attraction or repulsion—of identification with or separation from others, things, the world. That those contrary impulses of attraction and repulsion are what I call Eros and Thanatos.

There is a poetry of Eros: of encounter and connection, of relatedness (across the abyss), even of reconciliation.

There is also a poetry of Thanatos, of separating off from the world, of isolating the self in its misery and mysteries.

* * *

In the Louvre, Watteau's *Voyage to Cythera* is hung across from his *Gilles*, the Pierrot figure. In *Voyage to Cythera* you see erotic transcendence being enacted—a series of couples, each of the two lovers forming a world of enclosure with their answering glances (I think of the forlornness of the speaker in Jarrell's "The Woman at the Washington Zoo"—the need for the male glance/gaze to confirm her existence).

And then, across the gallery, the same painter's *Gilles*, the Pierrot, frontally confronting the viewer with his existential solitude. The self at that point where the ground of being shifts under its feet and solitude gives way to forlornness. Here the self is aware of its anxiety, alienated from the world, unable to transcend the conditions of its being.

* * *

In Petrarch's *Secretium,* his private self-examination where Saint Augustine interrogates him, Saint Augustine sneers at Laura's body being worn-out with illness and childbirth. Petrarch responds, yes, but she cleansed my youth and taught me to look upward. Augustine: "Nonsense! She has ruined your life! She turned you from the love of the Creator to the love of the creature!"

The Creator is supposed to be *up* there—the only true vertical. The Provençal lyric puts the Beloved up there, hopelessly high, and so she becomes a spiritual rather than a carnal aspiration.

But Blake says: the most sublime act is to place another before you. (Before, not above.)

And what does this idealizing accomplish? What need does it speak to? A need for something more, something beyond this "muddy stream" of "real things" Keats talks about; some bright star by which we can steer. "Love is an ever-fixed mark. . . ." The need to worship: "I must kneel to rise. . . ."

The struggle to bring the love-object down into the world (temporal beatitude); to worship the Terrestrial rather than the Celestial Venus.

* * *

> God appears and God is Light
> To those poor Souls who dwell in Night
> But does a Human Form Display
> To those Who Dwell in Realms of day.
> > Blake, "Auguries of Innocence"

* * *

Panofsky on the Four Humors. Melancholy, frenzy, Aristotle. How I love Aristotle over Plato, the scientific over the mythical, because "solider Aristotle" brings us back to bodies—

black bile, too much air in the blood making the melancholics lecherous, swelling their members (Problem XXX). I prefer that to Plato, who is too much like Worringer—the urge to abstraction motivated by an instinctive terror of the contingent, and a transcendent reaching for the abstract, the antilife (rock and crystal).

* * *

Blake tells us that the Abstract enslaves. When deities are abstracted away from the sensible objects into which Poetic Genius has projected them, then that is the beginning of Priesthood and mystification. He urges the "minute particulars." He locates the transcendent in the human body: "all deities reside in the human breast." The body has wisdom in Blake, a sexual wisdom: "the lineaments of gratified desire." The priests, with their "Thou Shalt Not" writ over the door of the Chapel of Love, are the enemy. They are cold; they "bind with briars my joys and desires."

Keats's body story is different than Blake's. He sees the body as a source of pleasure and of pain—he's a doctor. He sees "fever" there in the body—fever and fret and death (many early deaths in his life, including his own foreknown). In "Ode on a Grecian Urn" his description of gratified desire, consummated sexuality is one of sorrow and mild pathology ("a heart high-sorrowful and cloyed, / A burning forehead and a parching tongue"). Nor does Keats reject transcendence on theoretical principles, but on practical ones: it doesn't work *all* the way—you only end up in the "Purgatory blind" of a half-transcended state: you end up not with the Moon on her throne, but lost in the "verdurous glooms and winding mossy ways." This inability to escape our condition is a "flaw" in happiness ("Epistle to John Hamilton Reynolds"). This failure betrays us twice: not only does it not get us up out of suffering into the world of Romance and nonmortal beings (the elfs and Faeries), but "it spoils the singing of the nightingale"—that is, it venoms our days, alienates us from the sensual world where we must live, if we live.

* * *

According to Adorno, "the ground of both art and theory, meanwhile, should be somatic. The body in its singular 'thisness' was the constant negation of vainglorious conceptuality; its suffering was an unceasing cry of agony for redemption. Both art and theory were, before all else, an 'echo' of this 'suffering' " (qtd. in Julian Roberts, *German Philosophy: An Introduction,* p. 277).

* * *

"And my 'medicine' was the thing that gained me entrance to . . . [the] secret gardens of the self. It lay there, another world, in the self. I was permitted by my medical badge to follow the poor, defeated body into those gulfs and grottos. And the astonishing thing is that at such times and in such places—foul as they may be with the stinking ischio-rectal abscesses of our comings and goings—just there, the thing, in all its greatest beauty, may for a moment be freed to fly for a moment guiltily about the room. In illness, in the permission I as a physician have had to be present at deaths and births, at the tormented battles between daughter and diabolic mother, shattered by a gone brain—just there—for a split second—from one side to the other, it has fluttered before me for a moment." (William Carlos Williams, *The Autobiography,* p. 288)

This image of the body and the lyric flight. I'd like to link it to Whitman's insistence on the body (Whitman was a wound-dresser in the Civil War: he's also seen the horrors of the body). Likewise, with Keats, another physician who insists on the sensuous. This anchoring in the body may give a locus for lyric longing (an origin for it) and it may give depth to the lyric poet's longing for flight and escape.

The lyric poet's heightened awareness of the body as the locus of the conditional world which he wishes to escape. (Yeats's image of the body as "a tattered coat upon a stick"). The more intensely the poet feels the body, the more intimately he knows it, the more he longs for that "flight" which is born out of the body's anguish.

* * *

Williams: a lyric spirit anchored by Aristotle. Quoting Dewey: "the local is the only universal, upon that all art builds," he quotes Aristotle. And thus saved from Plato, saved from transcendence. Instead, the spiritual in the local: temporal beatitude.

III

Some Poets

A Reading of Donald Hall's "Kicking the Leaves"

When William Carlos Williams, in "A Sort of Song," calls on metaphor to "reconcile / the people and the stones," he clearly means by stones the world we inhabit, the world we move through. In that same lyric, Williams proposes a vegetative metaphor for the self, for his self: "Saxifrage is my flower that splits / the rocks." The vitality, almost stubborn muscularity of the metaphor is unmistakable and characteristic. Donald Hall's ambition in his major poem, "Kicking the Leaves," is also expressed through a metaphor from the vegetative world, but Hall's poem aims to reconcile us not to life (Williams's goal) but to death: lives are leaves.

"Kicking the Leaves" is a poem of family—four generations of Hall's personal family inhabit its seven sections. But it also belongs to the family of poems. At the source of the poem's unspoken genealogy, its genealogy of imagination, is Homer's famous metaphor from *The Iliad*, where Glaucos, challenged to identify himself by Diomedes, responds:

> Magnanimous Diomedes, why do you ask who I am? The frail generations of men have scarcely more lineage than leaves. Wind blows them to earth in the fall, but spring brings the blossoms again. So one generation succeeds another.

Published in the *Iowa Review* (1988) and in *The Day I Was Older: On the Poetry of Donald Hall*, edited by Liam Rector (Santa Cruz: Story Line Press, 1989).

A second sponsor of the leaf metaphor is Hopkins's "Spring and Fall," whose "leaves like the things of man" is the central imaginative premise for a poem of great elegiac beauty enacted as a child's dawning awareness of the mortality she shares with the world of created beings. But Hopkins's poem, unlike the passage from Homer, is also about human connectedness and awareness of others. For me, the pivotal line in the poem is "And yet you will weep and know why," where the young girl's emotional simplicity breaks through the speaker's self-satisfied philosophizing and demands a more authentic response, one that acknowledges and incorporates the deepest sources of her grief. Hall's poem shares with Hopkins's this awareness of other selves.

Leaves. Their very multiplicity, their "droveness," seems to resist transformation into a symbol of the human condition. As if we were accustomed to the lyric symbol which thrives on the precise outline of a single, centered thing—a nightingale, say. It is their resistance, their multiplicity, that is a form of the poem's generosity. Though the poem's sections tell the story of the generations of Hall's family and of his own life in time from boyhood to age, there is in the image of the multiplicity of leaves a clear sense that Hall is saying: I am only one leaf among all the leaves of human stories. We are half a step from Whitman's central invitation: "what I assume you shall assume, / For every atom belonging to me as good belongs to you."

Hall's generosity, his overcoming of the egocentrism that overwhelms so many lyric enterprises, is not his only accomplishment. As deep as that is his ability to hold the poem together so that it doesn't disperse into drifts and scuds. He does this by staying close to human story—to located anecdote. The poem is anchored in story and anecdote, yet opens up again and again toward mystery, toward the ultimate human mysteries of time and death.

It's not exactly news that the central impulse in Donald Hall's work is elegiac—that he is obsessed with elegy as others are said to be obsessed with sex or death. But it is worth noting that "Kicking the Leaves" is the triumphant culmination of this obsession. All his earlier, scattered elegiac occasions are, like raked leaves, gathered in one place: the beloved maternal grandparents and their farm, the father's early death that terrifies the son as predictive of his own, the ambivalent sense of his children's vitality and futurity, and there at the center the self longing to elegize its own perishing and be lifted up into elegy as certain saints were taken up bodily into heaven at the point of death. The poem opens with the long, accumulating, Whitmanic lines that will characterize it as a whole. The first sentence is seven lines long; the second sentence comprises the remaining ten lines of the section.

The initial verb, "kicking," is repeated four times in section one, becoming at the outset the incantatory gesture that initiates the poem's discoveries. The first occasion of kicking the leaves locates the speaker in a moment and place (October, Ann Arbor). The second "kick" leads to an awareness of particular leaves (maple, poplar, elm) and a tentative metaphorical listing. With the third repetition, the poem enacts its central process—the rising up of lost or buried memories and experiences by way of an unconsciously repeated gesture, the emergence of the "involuntary memory" Proust asserted as being central to urgent art. The sound of kicking the leaves triggers associated memories that transport us into three places in Hall's past: walking to school as a boy in Connecticut, roadside New Hampshire, and finally Massachusetts in 1955. We are always located geographically in section one, and these four places are and will remain the poem's cardinal points.

We could say the language unfolds under the momentum of the sound and gesture of the repeated "kick," until each sentence arrives at the poem's obsessive center: death. The listing of specific leaves and their metaphors gets no further than three, stops (as does the sentence) at the elm's, whose fatal blight occasions the metaphor. Likewise the second sentence, with its unfolding memories, also ends with the awareness of the father's impending death.

How the poem accumulates and accretes by its dependent clauses—"from the game, in Ann Arbor, / on a day the color of soot, rain in the air." If this was sculpture, Hall's style would be that of a modeler, not a carver; rather than stripping away toward a lyric center, he slaps on phrase after phrase like lumps of clay, building his shape gradually, each phrase adding, modifying, locating—always locating and making local. How powerfully that strategy is at work in the opening of section 2:

> Each fall in New Hampshire, on the farm
> where my mother grew up, a girl in the country

Section 2 is structured around two anecdotes. The general ("Each fall . . .") segueing into the particular ("One November . . ."), even as the grandson replaces his mother and thus preserves the basic family unit with the grandparents. People at work, moving around each other at their tasks—achieving an intimacy and harmony based on proximity and shared labor:

> three of us sitting together, silent, in gray November.

And always the clauses and phrases—clustering, accumulating, layering like leaves, modifying—here undercutting, there aggrandizing—always going on and on—a poem built on commas.

In section 2 the leaves are a minor, naturalistic part of the farm's dynamic life. They have a function—to insulate the house in winter, preserve its heat. In this section the reader becomes aware of how much of the poem relies on the power of descriptive language.

Section 3 presents another triadic anecdote, again particularized by its prepositional phrases: "One Saturday when I was little, before the war . . ." The whole anecdote/section is a single sentence, revealing the unity of the poem's stylistic and thematic strategy: to bind together in a single unit of speech the disparate figures and facts—a wholeness out of the bits of bright fact and memory, the scattered remnants of mortality— leaves gathered up into the single pile of the sentence.

The anecdote of this triad (father, son, mother) is of an interactive intimacy, not just the silent parallel labor of section 2. The father plays with the son, makes contact with him; the mother "sees" them and responds with both pleasure and concern. Since this is elegy, concern has the final word: "afraid I would fall and be hurt."

Section 4 returns to the opening scene of section 1, echoing the opening phrase: "Kicking the leaves today, as we walk home together." Now the poem's guiding, overarching metaphor begins to assert itself: the connections between the human world and the world of leaves. The stepping stone to this is the football pennants "as many and bright as leaves." From there to the third triadic arrangement of people: father (speaker), daughter, and son. People are like trees: the daughter like a birch; the son a maple. Again, we have the triad of a basic family unity, but here the speaker, for all his joy and pride in his children (expressed in the flattery of the similes), is about to become the locus of loss. The triad is not that of the child (speaker) and two parents (section 3) or the youth (speaker) and his grandparents (section 2), where the focus was on the child. Here it is the speaker as parent and his two children, and their futurity points away from him as the point of origin. It is an "unstable" triangle, a triad of imminent loss.

Sentence 1 (nine and a half lines) culminates in the grown son's eagerness to depart the family. Sentence 2 (the next nine lines, the rest of the section) focuses on the father ("I") as he experiences the vertigo of loss. Standing by a totem pile of leaves, he watches their departure ("their shapes grow small with distance") and recognizes in it his own diminishment and mortality. In an early, grimly elegant and witty poem, "My Son, My Executioner," the "birth" of one generation was seen as representing the death of the other, parental generation and gave a sinister, darkly Freudian undertone to Hall's elegiac impulse. But here, in "Kicking the Leaves," we are outside in the sun and fresh air of autumn, not trapped in the claustrophobic lucubrations of the self alone with its thoughts in a closed house. Here, the intimations of mortality are seen and accepted: "as I go first / into the leaves, taking / the step they will follow."

At first, "into the leaves" seems a euphemism for "into the ground," "into the grave," but it is one of the poem's burdens and triumphs to make a descent into the leaves as believable an imaginative possibility as it was when first presented to us in section 3 as the naturalistic possibility of a kid tumbling in leaves with his father. By section 6, the leaves will become the entrance to the underworld of the dead. And by section 7, they will have expanded to become not just a pile of leaves, but an entire ocean—an elemental, the elemental entity and emblem for the human condition of mortality, as all pervasive and insisted upon as Whitman's grass in his great celebratory elegy, *Song of Myself.*

The opening line of section 5 picks up and transforms the last line/gesture of section 1; here, instead of the father's death, we have the "birth" of poems, the "rebirth" of poems and creativity.

Sections 5 and 6 break the pattern of the long opening sentence—in fact, the first lines of both sections are end-stopped sentences.

For the first time, the poem shifts away from family memory and family event by introducing the theme of poetry: "This year the poems came back, when the leaves fell." One purpose of elegy is to articulate a loss and then locate a consolation for that loss. Although "Kicking the Leaves" has extended its elegiac ambition widely (and will, by poem's end, extend it even further), the end of section 4 has temporarily focused the imminent loss in the person of the speaker himself—it is he who will "go first / into the leaves." From this loss that is one's own death emerges the consolation that has always created and defined the personal poet: poems.

Only at the very moment that this consolation asserts itself most strongly ("I looked up into the maples / and found them, the vowels of bright desire") can the speaker acknowledge the horror of the years without poems. The image for this horror, a ghoulish mynah bird/rooster, is ironically located—up among the trees whose leaves are associated with poems, but the branches are bare, and such a sinister bird seems equally at home in the deathful confinement of chicken wire and cinder block, is in fact at home everywhere, haunting and taunting the speaker with its "red eye with no lid."

If there was any question that the poet's companion bird was an image of life without poems (which is also, the poem would have it, death-in-life), then this is resolved when the word "lid" is repeated three lines after its first appearance with the bird, only now, in the opening lines of section 6, it is the lid of a grave.

The red eye is now lidded, but the lids are of graves and the poem, while returning to the family (this time the paternal lineage) will impinge more fatefully than ever on the speaker. Section 6 seems to assert in an understated way a theory of generational diminishment (grandfather dies at seventy-seven, father at fifty-two) and a geographical diminishment as well (from farm to suburbs). These twin diminishments haunt the poet: Johnson's Pond has "surrendered to houses" and the speaker is now intensely aware of approaching the age at which his father died. Numerological doom presides over this section even as the ecstasy of nostalgic intimacy erupts through the middle:

> Oh, how we flung
> leaves in the air! How they tumbled and fluttered around us,
> like slowly cascading water, when we walked together

The final section takes its cue from the ecstatic verbs of section 6, not its gloomy numbers. The wisdom of verbs espoused here is reminiscent of that in Galway Kinnell's "Another Night in the Ruins"—if we are to be consumed by the fire, we should embrace it and become the fire. But Kinnell's poem, despite its overt rejection of the phoenix as emblem of the self, still believes in a transformation event at the moment of death—the transcendent ascent of annihilation implicit in his governing image of fire. Hall's poem refuses transformation, stays in the human shape, and asserts a descent. The three verbs in the opening line propound a metaphysics of passionate defeat in which gravity (and death) gets two verbs and the human will gets one: "Now I fall, now I leap and fall."

Or we could understand the phrasing as being a statement ("Now I fall") which the poet corrects even as he says it in order to express that his death is not a fate but a willed act: "now I leap and fall."

And the motive for such a gesture is revealed as intensified life: "to feel . . . to feel."

Now the leaves are everything. Now the leaves that represent the mortal condition are omnipresent—they are night and ocean, a cosmic, solemn, ecstatic vastness into which the individual self is absorbed. We have entered Whitman's imaginative territory here—the shadow Whitman of rapturous elegies whose "Out of the Cradle Endlessly Rocking" finds the sweetest word, the most "delicious" world of all, to be what the waves whisper: "death, death, death, death, death."

As with Whitman's poem, there is a sense of death as a being taken back—Hall experiences the death as an ecstatic regression, "the soft laps of leaves." And in fact, as he swims down to the bottom of the leaf pile he discovers his grandparents' farmhouse. Its enclosed intimacy has become all things: womb, tomb, beloved place of childhood. In a series of essays called *Seasons at Eagle Pond* (Ticknor and Fields, 1987), Hall writes of the joy of New England winters for those who are "darkness-lovers," those who are "partly tuber, partly bear" (Hall has an early poem called "Self-portrait, As a Bear"), and both ingredients of the farmhouse soup, carrots and onions, mature in the earth. Here dormancy and hibernation and cozy security fuse with nostalgia, and we see that the poem has adopted a strategy Freud recommends and which Hall frequently quotes: regression in the service of the ego. Roethke did the same thing throughout his "Lost Son" sequence—elevated regression to a spiritual and poetic principle.

Part of another Whitman poem, section 6 of *Song of Myself*, is worth mentioning in connection with this culminating event of Hall's poem. Significantly, it is the section in which Whitman first introduces the image of grass as a vehicle for his obsessive concerns, as that thing in the material world that will stand for so much in his metaphysical and imaginative world. It opens "A child said, *What is the grass?* fetching it to me with full hands." No sooner does Whitman express his inability to answer the mystery of the question with descriptive language than he begins to "guess" what it is with a series of stunning and free-ranging metaphors: a flag, perfumed handkerchief, child, universal hieroglyph. Free-ranging up to a point; for when he arrives at a certain image ("and now it seems to me the beautiful uncut hair of graves"), he has encountered an obsessive theme. From that point on, Whitman's imagination circles around one of his favorite subjects: a sensual death. Whitman has entered a spiral of obsession—his imagination is no longer free and centrifugal and, for the next twenty-six lines, he circlingly descends toward his still point of obsession and the poem's final line: "And to die is different from what anyone supposed, and luckier."

Hall, too, in the final section of "Kicking the Leaves," has entered the spiral of obsession; he, too, is drawn down as if in a whirlpool—"Swooping in long glides to the bottom."

Leaves are Hall's sea, not grass as in Whitman. There is no implied rebirth here, no hint of reincarnation no matter how diffuse, no "if you want me again look for me under your boot-soles." In Hall, the image of leaves, like Hopkins's Goldengrove that "leafmeal lies," cannot be imagined as leading beyond death. Presumably, Hopkins's Christianity tells him that death is not the end, that the soul rises afterward. Hall has no such faith, and for him the final ecstatic celebration of leaves and death is inextricably bound up with the consoling regressive fantasy of the farmhouse at the very bottom of the whirlpool's funnel—a personal and particular focus of intimacy. The image of this whirlpool spiral is important: it indicates that death is not a scattering of the objects and meanings of life, but a centripetal funneling, an ingathering of them.

Hall's poem accepts but transforms Homer's great metaphor. The generations of men are as leaves. But one can give assent—can leap as well as fall—the heroic acceptance of destiny. One could even argue that the Homeric consolation of leaving a name in the tribal epic through heroic behavior is also a consolation Hall's poem seeks: "the pleasure, the only long pleasure, of taking a place / in the story of leaves." But it would be important to stress the central feel of Hall's poem: not Homer's heroic warriors, but family intimacy and connection; a constant linking across generations, as families can do, as leaves and warriors cannot.

The Poems of Stanley Kunitz

If Stanley Kunitz is a major poet, then he must have a major theme. What is that theme? Something that for the moment I'll call "the son's quest for the father." As all authentic major themes of this century must, it represents a fusion of personal crisis with an impersonal universal significance. For the process of fusing personal and impersonal, the phrase Kunitz uses in relation to his own work is "to convert life into legend." I would assert that there must be a certain balance between the personal and impersonal in such an endeavor. In terms of the father-quest theme, Kunitz's early work (*Selected Poems*) is weighted toward the impersonal, and it is only in *The Testing Tree* that the poems approach the unadorned personal source. With the extraordinary simplicity and understatement that is his genius in the later work, he tells us the most essential tale of his life and his work:

> My mother never forgave my father
> for killing himself,
> especially at such an awkward time
> and in a public park,
> that spring
> when I was waiting to be born
>
> ("The Portrait")

Let us not underestimate how difficult such simplicity of statement is, nor how great a struggle Kunitz must go through before he can achieve such a straightforward telling of what

---

American Poetry Review (1979).

he elsewhere calls "the curious legend of my youth" ("Open the Gates").

Now that I've spoken of the personal source, the private source, now that I've applied such a grand label as "the son's quest for the father," what is it that this theme might mean to a reader who does not share the personal crisis that gave rise to it? Kunitz's quest for the father is no less than a quest for his identity. In a world where forces conspire constantly to destroy our individual sense of identity, a poet's struggle to discover (or create) and affirm his identity is a representative human struggle. If he is triumphant in his quest to affirm his own being in a confrontation with loss and death, then our sense of self is enhanced.

People seek the biological and psychological sources of their being in order to understand who they are. But in Kunitz's case, this quest for the biological and psychological source must confront at the very beginning of life the ultimate contradiction of human meaning: death, and self-willed death at that. This quest for the father is by definition—at least in terms of the physical world—doomed to utter failure. So it is removed to the level of the imagination (or legend) because the impossibility of the task does not affect the necessity of the quest. One must have meaning. In Kunitz's case, the quest for the meaning of his personal existence, his being, is intimately, biologically tied up with nonbeing. And this nonbeing is mysterious because it is surrounded by silence, because (on the literal level) who can say why someone commits suicide?

The theme of the quest for the father takes numerous forms in the body of Kunitz's work. We might start by saying that it is there at the beginning, in the earliest poem Kunitz includes in *The Poems of Stanley Kunitz 1928–1978,* "Vita Nuova." And it is there at the end, explicitly in the next-most-recent poem, "What of the Night?," and implicitly in the most recent, "The Knot." One can say, in terms that Kunitz himself might employ, that the theme of the son and the father is the alpha and omega of Kunitz's poetic vision.

In his first appearance, the father is simply part of a quest that we, as readers, participate in, but whose source and motive we don't understand. The speaker in "Vita Nuova" announces that a certain level of personal spiritual accomplishment will be achieved when he "wears his father's face":

> Now I will peel that vision from my brain
> Of numbers wrangling in a common place,
> And I will go, unburdened, on the quiet lane
> Of my eternal kind, till shadowless
> With inner light I wear my father's face.
>
> ("Vita Nuova")

Why this should be the culmination of a quest for identity we do not know, though it works well in the imagistic context. What the speaker seeks is a single self among the multiple selves (this single self to "wear the father's face"); perhaps this self is a growing outward of the "gentle self" within his external physical self (this is not necessarily clear). The other touchstone of all Kunitz's work that is present in "Vita Nuova" is intensity: the final word of the poem, its final aspiration is "intense":

> My dark will make, reflecting from your stones,
> The single beam of all my life intense.

Intensity will be the standard by which Kunitz measures all language and all statement in his poetry.

The title itself, from Dante's *Vita Nuova,* points to the physical death of a loved one as the moment of spiritual rebirth (or birth to the spiritual) of the survivor. Dante's poem is at the source of all poems of human loss which look forward (spiritual allegory) rather than backward (elegy).

I have already posited that a primary source of Kunitz's art is personal trauma, specifically the mysterious and violent death of his father and the ensuing quest that death imposed. In much of the early poetry that source is recognized and yet held at a considerable distance. Given the literary-historical context of the times (for example, Eliot's essays, where he propounds a theory of "impersonality" in poetry), the distance is not unusual, but the recognition of the personal, traumatic source is. Kunitz's early esthetic necessitated seeking a

99

more distant and objective set of images and narrative structures in which to speak of his personal crisis. What Kunitz didn't do (and here he resembles Roethke and Crane) is adopt any particular orthodoxy (either political and religious) whose dogma would provide formal resolutions to his dilemma and his poems without necessarily resolving them emotionally or thematically.

While rejecting orthodoxies, Kunitz turned to the literary, religious, and occult traditions and to science as a source of images. To provide a dramatic structure for his work at the deepest level, he put forward the notion of the poem as a spiritual allegory (my term not Kunitz's). The obvious "master" from whom one would derive such a notion is Dante. Another source for the poem's task and its link to the poet's life is Keats's remark (in a letter of May 3, 1819) that "the common cognomen of this world among the misguided and superstitious is a 'vale of tears' from which we are to be redeemed by a certain arbitrary interposition of God and taken to Heaven—what a little circumscribed straightened notion! Call the world if you please 'the vale of Soul-making.' " The poet's task is dynamic: he must create his own soul through the imagination, and the poems are the chronicle of this process. That is the central theme of the poet of imagination. Keats, Blake, and Yeats are avatars.

There is an old critical saw about Kunitz's poetry: that one prefers the earlier work (*Selected Poems*) or the later work (*The Testing Tree* and after). If I acknowledge my awe and admiration for the later work, it is not to denigrate the earlier achievement, but simply to say that I think it better fulfills its ambitions of tragic stance and intensity. Kunitz himself might be inclined this way since he has arranged the poems in reverse chronological order, so that we encounter the most recent poems first.

If the discussion of early Kunitz versus later Kunitz is reduced to stylistic preference on the reader's part—formal verse as opposed to free verse, high style versus "possible speech"—then a simplistic injustice is being done to the work as a whole. There is a stylistic shift, but more deeply than that there is a fundamental shift in Kunitz's relation to the world and to his life. If the earlier poems were often structured as intense, lyricized metaphysical and intellectual allegories whose discoveries and dramas involved transcending the physical world, then the later work is marked by a deep shift toward acceptance of the physical world and the existence of others. The intensity of many early Kunitz poems is the intensity of passionate intellect, but later work opens itself to a new world of feeling. I think of such a pivotal line as Wordsworth's "a deep distress hath humanized my soul" (*Elegiac Stanzas*) as being adequate to the absolute quality of the shift in Kunitz's sensibility, but with two important differences. There is a sense that for Wordsworth this change coincided with the onset of an emotional rigidity, whereas the opposite is true for Kunitz. Likewise, there was an immediate, traumatic incident that Wordsworth refers to (his brother's death by drowning), whereas there is no equivalent incident identifiable in Kunitz's work at the time. That incident which one might justifiably locate as the major source and well-spring of Kunitz's work (his father's suicide) is known to Kunitz and his work from the very start. One might speculate that there is a change in his treatment of the theme, his attitude toward it, but only in the sense that there is a change in his attitude toward everything, there is an opening toward the world of feeling and the world of people. The rules of existence stay the same; the human condition is still tragic, there is no final resolution possible to the suffering or the spiritual craving. As the moon-walking astronaut says in "Apollo":

> I know what I know: I shall never escape from
> strangeness or complete my journey. Think of me as
> nostalgic, afraid, exalted.

Although the son's quest for the father manifests itself at crucial moments in numerous earlier poems, the theme is best explored in two individual poems where it dominates the entire dramatic situation: "Father and Son" and "Open the Gates."

Father and Son

Now in the suburbs and the falling light
I followed him, and now down sandy road
Whiter than bone-dust, through the sweet
Curdle of fields, where the plums
Dropped with their load of ripeness, one by one.
Mile after mile I followed, with skimming feet,
After the secret master of my blood,
Him, steeped in the odor of ponds, whose indomitable love
Kept me in chains. Strode years, stretched into bird;
Raced through the sleeping country where I was young,
The silence unrolling before me as I came,
The night nailed like an orange to my brow.

How shall I tell him my fable and the fears,
How bridge the chasm in a casual tone,
Saying, "the house, the stucco one you built,
We lost. Sister married and went from home,
And nothing comes back, it's strange, from where she goes.
I lived on a hill that had too many rooms:
Light we could make, but not enough of warmth,
and when the light failed, I climbed under the hill.
The papers are delivered every day;
I am alone and never shed a tear."

At the water's edge, where the smothering ferns lifted
Their arms, "Father!" I cried, "Return! You know
The way. I'll wipe the mudstains from your clothes;
No trace, I promise, will remain. Instruct
Your son, whirling between two wars,
In the Gemara of your gentleness,
For I would be a child to those who mourn
And brother to the foundlings of the field
And friend of innocence and all bright eyes.
O teach me how to work and keep me kind."

Among the turtles and the lilies he turned to me
The white ignorant hollow of his face.

It is a most direct telling of the quest; a poem of seeking and beseeching. The father is called "the secret master of my blood." This is Kunitz's primary situation: the incredible urgency of the speaker and the impossibility of what he seeks. First, the pursuit (stanza 1); then the son's account of his life, "my fable and my fears" (stanza 2). What the father made ("the house, the stucco one") has been lost, a bad omen for the son (who was also "made" by the father) that is shown to be an accurate prediction two lines later with the house ("I lived on a hill"). There is a failure there for the son ("light we could make, but not enough of warmth")—a failure of feeling, an inadequacy of feeling. In stanza 3 the son's motive for the pursuit emerges: he believes that the father "knows the way," that he can instruct his son as fathers ordinarily do, are expected to do. The terms of aspiration that the speaker expresses (child, brother, then friend) recapitulate human growth from infancy to family link to adulthood: all that has been lost because of the absence of the father and his instructions. It is when this situation of beseeching has reached its peak of poignancy that the horrible, sudden resolution of the final two lines occurs. The father's face is "ignorant" (the knowledge cannot come from this source), "hollow" (the decay of death is real): both facts are revealed in the final physical gesture of the father's turning back at the last moment before he disappears under the surface of the pond. It is a moment of ghastly revelation, perhaps ironically heightened by the presence of "turtles" and "lilies"— both with biblical overtones germane to the poem.

Open the Gates

Within the city of the burning cloud,
Dragging my life behind me in a sack,
Naked I prowl, scourged by the black
Temptation of the blood grown proud.

Here at the monumental door,
Carved with the curious legend of my youth,
I brandish the great bone of my death,
Beat once therewith and beat no more.

The hinges groan: a rush of forms
Shivers my name, wrenched out of me.
I stand on the terrible threshold, and I see
The end and the beginning in each other's arms.

Again we have that incantatory energy that animates Kunitz's best work. "Father and Son" is a rather straightforward telling of his tale (minus one crucial detail: the suicide) in which he expresses his personal anguish and his imaginative link of the anguish to his father's absence. "Open the Gates" is that "quest" tale told at a mythic, Blakean level, with almost no personal contamination. (I say "almost": I think the meaning of the line "curious legend of my youth" is only fully revealed by the later poem, "The Portrait"). "Open the Gates" is a poem of archetypal vision and yet the whole thing is anchored by, suffused with and emanating a strange sexual energy. The final two lines represent a fusion of Apocalypse (the opening of St. John's *Revelation:* Alpha and Omega) and Freud's Primal Scene. Kunitz somehow witnesses, even participates in his own engendering.

I've said that I believe the major theme in Kunitz's work is the quest for the foundations of one's being. Because of the "curious legend" of Kunitz's youth, when Kunitz turns to the biological source (which is also the spiritual/metaphysical source) he confronts a mysterious absence that becomes a haunting, obsessive presence.

Sometimes this seeking leads to spiritual fathers who might also guide and instruct Kunitz, for example, Dante in "The Illumination" and Lincoln in "The Lincoln Relics."

At other times, the father's ghost or some analogue is the active seeker, and the speaker (Kunitz) is either passive or pursued. I would call this version of the story "the mysterious summons." We find an example in the early poem "Revolving Meditation":

> But why do I wake at the sound,
> In the middle of the night,
> Of the tread of the Masked Man
> Heavy on the stairs,
> And from the street below
> The lamentation of the wounded glove?

Or these lines from the next-most-recent poem, "What of the Night?," lines that are also linked to the father:

> What wakes me now
> like the country doctor
> startled in his sleep?
> Why does my racing heart
> shuffle down the hall
> for the hundredth time
> to answer the night bell?
> Whoever summons me has need of me

In yet another version of the story, Kunitz's father appears as an apparition:

> Bolt upright in my bed that night
> I saw my father flying;
> the wind was walking on my neck,
> the windowpanes were crying.
>
> ("Three Floors")

This child's vision of his father flying about in his bedroom is so similar to the apparition of Lincoln that Kunitz describes in "The Lincoln Relics" that it further confirms the link in Kunitz's imagination between his father and Lincoln:

> In the Great Hall of the Library,
> as in a glass aquarium,
> Abe Lincoln is swimming around,
> dressed to the nines
> in his stovepipe hat
> and swallowtail coat

A third and far more mythic form that the father takes in Kunitz's work is that of a tree in the "ancestral wood." Here the father is more likely to be grand, a kind of fusion of stag, oak, and vegetation deity as in section 3 of "The Way Down":

> O father in the wood,
> Mad father of us all,
> King of our antlered wills,
> Our candelabrum-pride
> That the pretender kills,
> Receive your dazzling child

In the marvelous poem "The Testing Tree" the father is both the tree the son confronts and a spirit whose blessing the son seeks for his ordeal:

> There I stood in the shadow,
>   at fifty measured paces,
>   of the inexhaustible oak,
> tyrant and target,
>   Jehovah of acorns,
>   watchtower of thunders,
> that locked King Philip's War
>   in its annulated core
>   under the cut of my name.
> Father wherever you are
>   I have only three throws
>   bless my good right arm.

Here we are in the imaginative territory of *The Golden Bough* with its rituals of struggle and renewal in the woods. This shows another imaginative level at which Kunitz's quest for the father can be apprehended. Related to the identification of the father with trees and vegetation deities is his association in Kunitz's imagination with ponds. The ultimate confrontation between father and son in "Father and Son" takes place as the father or his ghost is entering a pond. In "Goose Pond," a "white-lipped boy" is born up from the pond and, as he climbs out on the bank, meets "his childhood beating back / To find what furies made him man." In the late poem "Quinnapoxet," Kunitz is fishing in an abandoned reservoir when he has a vision of his father and mother approaching him. In "The Testing Tree," a recurring dream has Kunitz look down a well at an albino walrus who has his father's gentle eyes. It's not necessary for us to understand why the father is associated with these different figures, situations, and natural phenomena: the important thing to recognize is that the theme of the father and the son's quest can take numerous forms.

In identifying the father's presence in various forms in various kinds of poems, I do not mean to be reductive. For one thing, Kunitz's father exists at the very start on the level of legend. Kunitz has no father in the sense that most people do, and so the word "father," which most people use concretely, is for Kunitz and Kunitz's work already a symbolic reality.

The Portrait

My mother never forgave my father
for killing himself,
especially at such an awkward time
and in a public park
that spring
when I was waiting to be born.
She locked his name
in her deepest cabinet
and would not let him out,
though I could hear him thumping.
When I came down from the attic
with the pastel portrait in my hand
of a long-lipped stranger
with a brave moustache
and deep brown level eyes,
she ripped it into shreds
without a single word
and slapped me hard.
In my sixty-fourth year
I can feel my cheek
still burning.

At first it might seem that we do not need to know the information contained in "The Portrait" in order to appreciate what Kunitz is about. And yet, we do. What is more, Kunitz needs to know this information, needs to introduce it into the body of his work. This is the pivotal poem in his whole work, the poem which makes possible the greatness of the later poems. When I say Kunitz needs to know, I mean that the poem acknowledges and integrates certain important pieces of information about his life, certain pieces until now missing from the puzzle. Without these pieces, Kunitz cannot hope to achieve his ambition of "converting life into legend." Now the essential elements of the "life" are present and a true growth can occur that is as rare and powerful as that of the later Yeats.

Not only do we learn for the first time that Kunitz's father was a suicide, but also that it was before Kunitz's birth, and perhaps most significantly, that Kunitz's mother "never forgave." For almost the first time, the mother appears and her role becomes clear. As long as Kunitz confined the dynamic of his imaginative life to Father-Son, it seemed impossible to go beyond simple seeking and confronting ("Father and Son"). But when he introduces the mother and her role, suddenly the possible dynamics are greatly extended. Soon other figures enter the poems: Frieda, Kunitz's daughter, his wife, the woman of "After the Last Dynasty," and others. All this is made directly possible by the mother's entrance.

For the first time it is not simply the father's death and mysterious absence that are seen to exert power over the whole of Kunitz's life. The mother's role in the persistence of suffering is revealed: it is her slap on his cheek that still burns fifty years or more later. The persistence of trauma is central to Kunitz's work: the struggle to be healed that takes a whole lifetime of imagination. This poem reveals that it is not simply the father's absence, but also the mother's rage that combine to trap the boy/adult Kunitz. Even later in Kunitz's work, the mother's slap ("my cheek / still burning") becomes the "gashed thumb" of the poem "Quinnapoxet." In "Quinnapoxet," Kunitz receives a wound from a fish in the "abandoned reservoir," this wound he shares with his father whose apparition approaches him "with his face averted / as if to hide a scald." It is the father's scald (the suicide wound) and Kunitz's hurt thumb that represent a link between father and son. Kunitz signals to his father:

> I touched my forehead
> with my swollen thumb
> and splayed my fingers out—
> in deaf-mute country
> the sign for father.

Even the form of Kunitz's wound, a "swollen thumb," has to do with a male, phallic life-force, a life-force "hurt" into being, yet potent. Through this shared wound (scald and gashed thumb) Kunitz does indeed fulfill in a strange way the prophecy of inheritance of that earliest poem, "Vita Nuova"; he does indeed "wear his father's face" (as he also did in the "burning cheek" of "The Portrait").

In the preceding discussion I've skipped ahead a little, skipped around. Let me reorient myself by quoting from a lecture Stanley Kunitz delivered at the Library of Congress on May 12, 1975, "From Feathers to Iron." Kunitz says:

> One of my convictions is that at the center of every poetic imagination is a cluster of key images which go back to the poet's childhood and which are usually associated with pivotal experiences, not necessarily traumatic. . . . That cluster of key images is the purest concentration of the self, the individuating node, the place where the persona starts. . . . In Keats' case, one can learn more about his quiddity by pursuing images of fever and of ooze than by analyzing his literary sources. A critical property of key images is that they are unalterable, being good for a lifetime.

In looking at Kunitz's poetry, two key images that I have noticed are 1) threshold/lintel and 2) a set of images clustered around the words *stain, wound, scald, burn, bleed*. I haven't the space here to explore the image of the threshold/lintel, except to say that it remains essentially itself and, in the final (most recent) poem, "The Knot," it becomes fused with the second key image. I hope to examine the second key image partly because it fascinates me by its metamorphoses: it evolves through the course of the work.

It makes its first appearances in the work as "hurt" (an abstraction) and as "stain" (a literary word):

> The blessing in this conscious fruit, the hurt
> Which is unanswerable, fill the brow
> With early death
>
> ("Beyond Reason")

> The shape confronting me upon the stair
> (Athlete of shadow, lighted by a stain
> On its disjunctive breast—I saw it plain—)
>
> ("Master and Mistress")

The stain of the second poem is associated with a ghost/apparition. The hurt of the first is associated with the brow. In later poems, the "hurt" will become less abstract, more violent and concrete, and increasingly associated with the head and brow. It is even at the outset an image of being soiled by mortality; but it is held at a distance, abstracted and intellectualized, even afraid of its own physical implications. This is appropriate to the early poetry, where a primary attitude is held in favor of Platonic forms and permanence as against the threatening flux of the physical world:

> Are the leaves red now? No matter
>   Trees are green.
>
> The colors of the world are permanent
> Despite the bleach of change. Pure stain on stain,
> the bow of light's eternal forms is bent
> Across steep heaven in the general brain . . .
>
>   ("Last Words")

Even here, where "stain" and purity are linked (as if to contradict my earlier hints) the stain is still associated with "brain," and the issue of mortality is present. In a poem called "The Pivot" this strange image occurs:

>   he leaves behind
>
> A faunlike head upon a tray,
> Spear buried in the mind.

In an early poem about poetry a "rhythmic Spike of Light" will "cleave" the brain.

    I don't want to be reductive (quite the opposite), but I want to establish that this pervasive set of images has an imaginative link to the father's probable method of suicide. We are not talking about what is seen or known, but what Kunitz imagines. We are looking at these images in the light of what we now know because of "The Portrait," but that seems legitimate to me. Perhaps it is unnecessary to continue this lesser list and we can move on to a more direct poem of the father-son dynamic and a more striking instance of this image complex.

There is a famous or notorious image in the poem "Father and Son." Critics have chided Kunitz for using "surrealism" in what would otherwise be a great poem. The immediate situation is that the son is pursuing the father across a landscape:

> Raced through the sleeping country where I was young,
> The silence unrolling before me as I came,
> The night nailed like an orange to my brow.

In one sense we realize that the orange is the moon. But isn't it also another and more striking version of the "stain" and "brow" images that we have seen earlier? Isn't it an emblem of the father's violent death that the questing son wears on his brow? We see this image again in "The Lincoln Relics," where the speaker addresses a Lincoln who in many ways is a spirit-father:

> Has no one told you
> how the slow blood leaks
> from your secret wound?

I've already mentioned the "burning cheek" of "The Portrait" and its connection to the "scald" on the father's averted face in "Quinnapoxet." Although the signaling of son's wound to father's wound in "Quinnapoxet," a very recent poem, is perhaps the most dramatic instance of the image complex, Kunitz saves the most fascinating for the first poem in his book *The Poems of Stanley Kunitz: 1928–1978,* "The Knot." Here he manages to fuse in imagination two of the key images in his work: a carved lintel and a persistent wound. The knot is a wood knot "scored in the lintel of my door." But like the persistent trauma of Kunitz's life and work, the knot constantly reasserts its presence. The word used to describe this reassertion is "bleeds." Bleeds is naturalistically correct for the phenomenon, but it also strongly suggests wound. The word "trauma" is used also. Since I wish to discuss this poem more fully in another context, I'll rest the case with the observation that the successful fusion of two key images is very important. It gets very close to the central theme of identity, since earlier in Kunitz's work we have heard of lintels or doorways that are carved with his name. In one important sense his name, his identity is that wound, that trauma, the violent source of his being.

The poem "The Portrait" contains a fourth crucial piece of information that relates directly to Kunitz's search for his identity. In lines 7–9, we see a link made between someone's name and their physical being:

> She locked his name
> in her deepest cabinet
> and would not let him out

Syntactically, those three lines have taken us from someone's name to their whole being. What we are being told on the literal level is that the boy Kunitz does not even know his father's name; what a resonant strangeness here. When in the poignant lyric "The Game" Kunitz says:

> O the night is coming on
> And I am nobody's son.

he means it literally: at the source of his being is a nameless absence. The word "name" is another of the "key images" of Kunitz's work. In the ritual confrontation in the woods of "The Testing Tree," the target oak he faces is carved with his name. His name is "wrenched out of him" in "Open the Gates." That terrible threshold that is sometimes carved with his name, sometimes marred by trauma, is the symbolic point of his entrance into the world: it is the doorway for his entrance into being that at his very birth is "carved with the curious legend."

To return briefly to the poem "Quinnapoxet," when Kunitz with his wounded hand signals to his father who averts his face to hide his "wound," he signals across the barrier of the mother. It was not simply the father's absence that crippled Kunitz and hindered his search for identity, but the mother's lack of "forgiveness." Not until she enters the story can we begin to hear the full notes of the other major theme of later Kunitz: love.

There are "love" poems before "The Magic Curtain." There are certainly poems of passion and passionate rhetoric addressed to women and partaking of all the attributes of the Western poetry of love. But how could Kunitz write poetry of love before he wrote a poem about his first love:

> At breakfast mother sipped her buttermilk,
>   her mind already on her shop
>   unrolling gingham by the yard,
> stitching her dresses for the Boston trade.
> Behind her, Frieda with the yellow hair,
>   capricious keeper of the toast,
>   buckled her knees, as if she'd lost
> balance and platter, then winked at me, blue-eyed.
> Frieda, my first love! who sledded me to sleep
>   through snows of the Bavarian woods
>   into the bell-song of the girls,
> with kinds of kisses mother would not dream

Nor am I being facetious when I say that Kunitz cannot write about love before he writes about love's beginnings. Kunitz of all poets must understand the importance of beginning and origins. And there at the beginning we find not only the first love, Frieda, but Kunitz's mother. At first the mother is only a little dour and serious, someone who must be outwitted so that the boy Kunitz and Frieda, the maid, can share their secret adventures at the cinema. But by the final section Kunitz's mother is, for love, the same negating power that she was for paternity in "The Portrait." "The Portrait" begins with that quietly intense phrase of negation: "my mother never forgave my father." Compare this with the concluding drama of "The Magic Curtain":

> when the film is broken, let it be spliced
>   where Frieda vanished one summer night
> with somebody's husband, daddy to a brood.
> And with her vanished, from the bureau drawer
>   the precious rose-enameled box
> that held those chestnut-colored curls
> clipped from my sorrowing head when I was four.

> After the war an unsigned picture-card
> from Dresden came, with one word: Liebe.
> "I'll never forgive her," mother said.
> but as for me, I do and do and do.

Again, the extraordinary negating power of the phrase "I'll never forgive." But this time Kunitz's affirmation in the last line of the poem is threefold: 1) he does forgive and thus repudiates his mother's stance, 2) he pronounces a marriage vow (I do) that pledges him to his first love and what she represents, and 3) he speaks to his German maid with the intimate form of "you" ("du"). What a triumphant ending to a beautiful poem.

In Kunitz's later work, loss/abandonment leads to love, brings forth love, whether that loss is Frieda or his father. How unlike Plath, for whom the father's loss brought rage and negation. There is something of this grim heritage in Berryman also. In "Dream Song 384" he feels a homicidal rage toward his already dead (from suicide) father; it is a grisly inversion of the father-son quest in Kunitz, and I would argue that the final legacy of Berryman's hatred is his own suicide.

Legacy of another sort is a central theme of "Journal for my Daughter." When "The Magic Curtain" opens the door to love, it also opens to the actual existence of other people. The self-enclosed world of much of Kunitz's earlier work is broken: both the world and other people begin to enter the poems and assert their own realities. In "Journal," the primary encounter is between Kunitz and his daughter by a previous marriage. For the first time, Kunitz faces toward the future generation rather than back toward his father. For once, he is the adult and not the child. This is an extremely important shift, because he now finds that he and his absence from his child's life are sources of her suffering; in other words, one theme of "Journal" is that Kunitz has almost passed on his own heritage/inheritance of misery. The poem begins with Kunitz "turning the platform over" to his daughter:

> Your turn, Grass of confusion.
> You say you had a father once;
> his name was absence.
> He left, but did not let you go.

How close this is to the situation of the absent father of "Father and Son" whose "indomitable love kept me [son] in chains." The daughter is haunted by the absent father, just as Kunitz was.

Section 2 presents a new, naturalistic Kunitz who can say:

> I wake to a glittering world,
> to the annunciation of the frost

Here is an early hint of Coleridge's "secret ministry of frost"—as we'll see later, Coleridge is a guiding presence in this poem. Suddenly the natural world is the adequate symbol or at least the right place to begin. Within the simplicity of the diction, the symbolic resides: this "waking" is more than physical:

> I propose
> that we gather our affections.
> Lambkin, I care.

The direct and simple speech suffices. The time has come to acknowledge all the human emotions, to trace the history of a life and a relationship (father-daughter) by reference to feelings: "I was happy you were born." The poem's shifts are the shifts of feeling: from "resentment" (section 1) to a counter-proposal of "affections" and "care" (section 2), to remembered happiness and present joy (section 3), to suffering ("You cried. You cried," section 4), to fear ("you crawled under the sofa," section 5).

There is in this poem an assertion of the primacy of feelings: of passion, desire, need. In section 6, Kunitz puts forward his "wisdom" in the opening lines:

> Goodies are shaken
> from the papa-tree:

> Be what you are. Give
> what is yours to give.
> Have style. Dare.
> Such a storm of fortune cookies!

He mocks his own need to communicate his wisdom to his daughter, his own pretensions (just as he mocks hers and later her generation's). The lines that follow present the most vivid nightmare image of the absent father who comes back to haunt his child (but this time the ghost is Kunitz, not his father):

> Outside your room
> stands the white-haired prowler
> in his multiple disguises
> who reminds you of your likeness.
> Wherever you turn,
> down whatever street,
> in the fugues of appetite,
> in the groin of nightmare,
> he waits for you

This is a poem about legacy and responsibility: Kunitz must accept responsibility for and attempt to overcome with affection the negative role he plays in his daughter's imagination. Section 6 concludes with another set of messages that parallel the fortune cookies of the opening. The first messages were gifts he wants to give, the last are assertions of his own needs and desires:

> What do I want of my life?
> More! More!

This emphatic repetition is extremely important in Kunitz's work as a kind of index of intensity. In "The Knot": "Let be! Let be!"; in "The Mulch": "Repeat. Repeat."

Section 7 continues the theme, brings it to its presentness in the 1960s—the protest demonstrations. Kunitz manages to affirm the demonstrations and still see them as that other

116

necessary dimension: the child's/young's rebellion against the parental generation:

> If your slogan is mis-spelt
> Don't tred on me!
> still it strikes
> parents and politicians down.
> Noli me tangere! is what
> I used to cry in Latin once.
> Oh to be radical, young, desirable
> cool!

"Noli me tangere"—"Touch me not!": indeed that is the banner under which we might have found the younger Kunitz, the earlier work.

Section 8 presents the death of the first pet and the child's authentic ambivalence toward death ("you sobbed / then romped"). This becomes the marker for the father's departure. The statement "It was the summer I left" is framed by two incidents: 1) the pet's death and burial, and 2) the father carrying the sleepy child outside to view an eclipse. Perhaps the pet's death represents both the entrance of tragedy into the child's world and the ability of the child's life-spirit to absorb that tragedy: to sob, then romp. This leads to that event in the world that will be harder to absorb: "It was the summer I left." When Kunitz carries his sleepy child outside immediately after, it becomes the last assertion of the parent-child relationship in all its tenderness and intimacy and also a mutual confronting of the mysteries of the world (although in the benign form of an eclipse).

It also brings us to section 9, a precisely analogous situation in which Coleridge ("heavy-hearted") carries his child out into the night. Coleridge is "heavy-hearted," his child is "crying": it is the mutuality of sorrow and suffering that is enacted, but at a distance from Kunitz and his daughter, as if to say, this is both personal to us and also shared by many humans. This is one of the deeper uses of transcendent moments: not to take us out of the world, but to momentarily lift the heaviness of the personal burden by recognizing the transpersonal within the personal. The poem ends on a perception:

> those brimming eyes
> caught the reflection
> of the starry sky,
> and each suspended tear
> made a sparkling moon.

The perception is exquisitely precise; it seems to stand in some ways as an arrested moment of feeling ("suspended tears") and intimacy, a magical communion. It's a characteristic gesture of Kunitz in poetry: to step aside, almost a kind of modesty toward the great poets and poems of the past as well as tenderness toward his daughter. He no longer seems so much to wish to transcend the real world, and yet he nevertheless is not completely comfortable in it, and he steps to the side at the very end and lets Coleridge seem to speak for him. The image is also an affirmation of change, of imagination: the tears of inner suffering and the light from the world make a third, a new thing, which is beautiful and mysterious.

"The Lincoln Relics" is one of the ultimate poems of Kunitz's father-son theme. Here that personal theme fuses with the less personal theme of the individual and the state. (I'd say Kunitz's three enduring themes are: father-son, love, and the individual and the state). Again the challenge is to affirm being in the face of nonbeing. Death, violence, and negation must be overcome by some authentic act of imagination and affirmation fused together. In section 1, Kunitz rejects the miracles associated with saints' relics and yet affirms the human spirit that Lincoln represents for him:

> Cold-eyed in Naples once,
> while the congregation swooned.
> I watched the liquefaction
> of a vial of precious blood,
> and wondered only
> how the trick was done.
> Saint's bones are only bones

> to me, but here,
> where the stage is set
> without a trace of gore,
> these relics on display—
> watchfob and ivory pocket knife,
> a handkerchief of Irish linen,
> a button severed from his sleeve—
> make a noble, dissolving music
> out of homely fife and drum,
> and that's miraculous.

The paradox that the Lincoln relics are homely and yet noble is what Kunitz chooses to affirm as "miraculous." We are in the territory of a spirit-father here: a legendary father, grand, mysterious, and martyred. I am not in any way trying to say Lincoln is merely a substitute for his father. What I mean is that Kunitz's past gives him a peculiar sensitivity to this situation of father figures who are heroic yet doomed, and who are genuinely worthy of our love. Kunitz has access to the theme because of his own "curious legend" and because of the way his imagination has transformed that legend. Again, Kunitz is an extraordinary human spirit in that he encounters at the start of his life a devastating negation and he overcomes (transforms and transfigures) that negation through a major and constantly renewed act of affirmative imagination.

Space doesn't permit me to examine this wonderful poem at length, but only to say that once again (as with so many of the later poems), there is a steady deepening of the father-son theme; it is for Kunitz an inexhaustible mine always capable of yielding new insights, new discoveries about the human spirit, if only he has the courage to dig deeper and deeper into it. As he says near the end of "The Testing Tree":

> It is necessary to go
>   through dark and deeper dark
>   and not to turn

I want to make only a minor observation about the conclusion of "The Lincoln Relics." Kunitz's own youth and old age are themes here: the quiet imminence of his own life's end as well

119

as the awareness that Lincoln is "slipping away from us into his legend and his fame." From this double desolation Kunitz's imagination spontaneously generates a new affirmation of the life spirit: the final section of the poem hints briefly at the possibility of Lincoln's reincarnation in a young man glimpsed in a crowd. In this way, the poem is a further stepping toward the future, a direction that we first encountered strongly in "Journal for My Daughter."

The Layers

I have walked through many lives,
some of them my own,
and I am not who I was,
though some principle of being
abides, from which I struggle
not to stray.
When I look behind,
as I am compelled to look
before I can gather strength
to proceed on my journey,
I see the milestones dwindling
toward the horizon
and the slow fires trailing
from the abandoned camp-sites,
over which scavenger angels
wheel on heavy wings.
Oh, I have made myself a tribe
out of my true affections,
and my tribe is scattered!
How shall the heart be reconciled
to its feast of losses?
In a rising wind
the manic dust of my friends,
those who fell along the way,
bitterly stings my face,
Yet I turn, I turn,
exulting somewhat,
with my will intact to go
wherever I need to go,
and every stone on the road

> precious to me.
> In my darkest night,
> when the moon was covered
> and I roamed through wreckage,
> a nimbus-clouded voice
> directed me:
> "Live in the layers,
> not on the litter."
> Though I lack the art
> to decipher it,
> no doubt the next chapter
> in my book of transformations
> is already written.
> I am not done with my changes.

At this point we are facing Kunitz's art stripped down to its essentials, and yet the poem contains everything his art is about. Here are the key situations and words all fused into one whole drama: "struggle," "being," the intensity of the spiritual allegory, "affections," affirmation out of deepest desolation, "transformation." All this and age as well. The final test of a poetry of this sort might be its ability to affirm in the face of personal death. We have moved even beyond that other great poem of age, "King of the River," whose final triumph was a series of intense paradoxes:

> forever inheriting his salt kingdom,
> from which he is banished
> forever.

In "The Layers," Kunitz moves past paradox into pure, strange statement: exultant, quiet, confident: "I am not done with my changes."

Has any poet of our time but Kunitz been equal to Yeats's self-admonition?

> Myself must I remake
> Till I am Timon and Lear
> Or that William Blake

> Who beat upon the wall
> Till Truth obeyed his call;
> . . . .
> Forgotten else by mankind,
> An old man's eagle mind.
>
> ("An Acre of Grass")

I spoke of "The Lincoln Relics" as fusing two themes of Kunitz's work. I would begin a discussion of "The Knot" by mentioning that it fuses the lintel and an analogue of the "stain/wound" image, the knot. There is also the serious pun of "knot" that plays off against the Gordian knot: that "puzzle" Alexander solved by slicing through, just as the "knot" in Kunitz's poem remembers its "lopping-off."

The Knot

> I've tried to seal it in,
> that cross-grained knot
> on the opposite wall,
> scored in the lintel of my door,
> but it keeps bleeding through
> into the world we share.
> Mornings when I wake,
> curled in my web,
> I hear it come
> with a rush of resin
> out of the trauma
> of its lopping-off.
> Obstinate bud,
> sticky with life,
> made for the rain again,
> it racks itself with shoots
> that crackle overhead,
> dividing as they grow.
> Let be! Let be!
> I shake my wings
> and fly into its boughs.

At the outset the attitude of the speaker toward the knot is ambivalent. The first (and priorly existing) impulse has been to seal it in, to repress it. By the poem's end, extraordinary changes have taken place, both in the knot itself and in the speaker's relationship to it. It emerges as a poem of dual metamorphosis, both the poem and the speaker. The speaker begins as a responsible, disapproving homeowner ("I've tried to seal it in, / that cross-grained knot / on the opposite wall"). By line 8 there is a hint of his metamorphosis during sleep ("curled in my web"—perhaps spider, and yet later womb connotations to "curled" will assert themselves as possible hints toward that most dramatic of metamorphoses, caterpillar into butterfly), by the next to last line of the poem, the speaker has wings. The speaker is not a bird, such a metamorphosis would be reductive, but intense change has taken place. The knot is as active, as dynamic as the "I" of the poem. It behaves as if its reduction from living tree branch to knot on a board had not occurred, or had not thwarted its life-force. What had been wound and trauma (the knot) is now a life-source; that very image of negation and death: the wound, has become the source of life. The knot asserts itself as a sexualized resurgence of such energy that by the poem's end the relative size and relationship of the poem's two characters have been reversed (human speaker to knot in board becomes bird to tree). The line "dividing as they grow" also brings in a strong sense of the rapid cell division of earliest, most intense biological development. The movement psychically has been from an original impulse toward suppression on Kunitz's part ("I tried to seal it in") to the speaker's being sheltered within its amplitude ("I shake my wings / and fly into its boughs").

Kunitz's "Let be! Let be!" has two meanings: the plea "Desist" and the plea "permit be-ing to exist intensely—permit me to be." How the energy of knot-into-tree triumphs, and yet Kunitz himself has the final triumph of a last metamorphosis ("I shake my wings") and a reconciliation with the recognition of his deep relationship to that very trauma/life-force (bird flying into tree boughs).

Kunitz's imagination has one purpose: to affirm being over nonbeing. But it is always a struggle. To read Kunitz rightly we must accept that there is a hurt, a negation, at the beginning of Kunitz's life that resonates and persists through the whole life and that affects all the important aspects of life. This negation is not only the primary negation of death (his father's suicide and the early death of the beloved stepfather telescoped together), but the secondary negation of the mother's unwillingness or inability to "forgive."

Kunitz's primary experience is loss or absence. This fixes a deeply sombre color to his experience of a primary reality: change. If change is real, it can be a negative change (death, nonbeing: the ignorant hollow) or positive, affirmative change (metamorphosis, transformation, other "triumphs" of imagination that fuse with being and the life-force). The stakes are high. When poets in our time have struggled with nonbeing, it has often ended badly: Berryman's suicide, Sylvia Plath's and Hart Crane's; Roethke's and Lowell's periodic bouts of madness. These poets express that confrontation with nonbeing that is a primary human encounter; we need to hear as much about it as possible, because we share it. As Hopkins concludes, addressing a child named Margaret who weeps over her first experience of leaves falling in autumn:

> It is the blight man was born for,
> It is Margaret you mourn for.
> ("Spring and Fall")

In "The Testing Tree," the boy Kunitz throws his stones at the target oak carved with his name in a magic ritual/gamble. If he is successful the prize is three forms of triumph of being over nonbeing: love, poetry (imagination), and eternal life. When in later poems he comes to embrace metamorphosis and leave behind the Platonic forms beloved by a more fearful early Kunitz, his notion of eternal life changes, becomes less desperate and conventional. A clear instance of this change is provided by the concluding lines of "The Guilty Man" as they appear in *Selected Poems:*

> Therefore depart from me you virtuous men
> Whose treason is to turn the conscience kind
> The souls of numbers kiss the perfect stars.

and those same final lines as they have been revised for the collected volume:

> So quit me now, you honorable men
> Whose treason is to turn the conscience kind,
> And do not turn until you hear a child.

Metamorphosis, desire, memory, vision, love, transformation, myths of quest, dream, will, revelation—it's as though each of the later poems puts forward another profound strategy of affirmation, another new way to endorse and participate in the life force and overcome the ever-present negation. It is not "himself" that he remakes in each of the later poems, it is the human spirit that he rebuilds from its foundations. He discovers, in "gathering strength to proceed on his journey" ("The Layers"), what resources the human spirit has at its disposal to affirm against the realities of negation and despair. It is not simply imagination that affirms. The ceaseless crisis of the spirit demands an affirmation of the whole being that requires great courage and dignity. Kunitz's work is deeply grounded in the tragic sense: an intense, simultaneous awareness of man's dignity and his weakness:

> In a murderous time
>   the heart breaks and breaks
>   and lives by breaking.
> It is necessary to go
>   through dark and deeper dark
>   and not to turn.

What we discover as we open ourselves more and more to Kunitz's work is that poetry can deal with the deepest issues of the individual human life. It is that triumphant endeavor we once hoped and believed it was. There is something of utmost human importance going on here. This is the poetry of the human spirit: matters of life and death and language: the spirit and the world fuse into one vision that affirms without falsifying.

The Need for Poetics
Some Thoughts on Robert Bly

1

Why does poetry matter? Is it important? If poets do not feel and think passionately about poetry how shall it be redeemed? Poets must write those essays about poetry that only poets can write: those in which blood is mixed with the ink. Keats's letters are an inexhaustible source of nourishment and guidance to young poets, to people beginning the enterprise and life of poetry. But poetry must be reaffirmed and reinterpreted by poets in each generation. Ezra Pound did this with his *ABC of Reading* and his essays (especially "A Retrospect" and "A Few Do's and Don't's of an Imagiste"). T. S. Eliot did likewise when he published "Tradition and the Individual Talent" in 1919. In regard to Eliot, it is interesting to note that shortly thereafter he began his own magazine, *Criterion,*

> the purpose of which was, he tells us, to create a place for the new attitudes to literature and criticism, and to make English letters a part of the European community. (Northrop Frye, *T. S. Eliot: An Introduction*)

The poet's role as reaffirmer and interpreter of the worth and purpose of poetry has declined since the great Moderns, but the strategies of that role—the essay, the magazine with a purpose—remain the same.

Appeared originally in *Poetry East* (1981); included in *Of Solitude and Silence: Writings on Robert Bly* (Boston: Beacon Press, 1981).

A critic can tell us what a poem means, but not what poetry means. The ethos of poetry is in the keeping of the poets in each generation, in each historical period. And not just as it is embodied in the best poems, but as the life of poetry is rendered in the intense and thoughtful forms of the essay, the statement of poetics, and the manifesto.

Why did so few American poets in the fifties write in the essay form about poetry? Perhaps in part this was a legacy of the New Critics, whose marvelous instruments of analysis too often left the poem in neatly sorted and labeled piles of sinew and viscera. Were the best poets cowed by these critics, rendered so self-conscious they ventured few and modest claims for their art?

> Most American poets of my generation were taught to admire the English Metaphysical poets of the seventeenth century and such contemporary masters of irony as John Crowe Ransom. We were led by our teachers and by the critics whom we read to feel that the most adequate and convincing poetry is that which accommodates mixed feelings, clashing ideas, and incongruous images. Poetry could not be honest, we thought, unless it began by acknowledging the full discordancy of modern life and consciousness. I still believe that to be a true view of poetry. (Richard Wilbur, *Poets on Poetry*, ed. Howard Nemerov)

Perhaps the poets of the fifties experienced that sense of social displacement that gives an undertone of insecurity and resentment to the lucid intelligence that animates Randall Jarrell's best essays. One might also think of the poets of that period as having suffered too much history, as in Louis Simpson's wonderful poem, "The Silent Generation," which rhythmically enacts the psychic disintegration it describes:

> When Hitler was the Devil
> He did as he had sworn
> With such enthusiasm
> That even, *donnerwetter*
> The Germans say, "Far better
> Had he been never born!"

> It was my generation
> That put the Devil down
> With great enthusiasm.
> But now our occupation
> Is gone. Our education
> Is wasted on the town.
>
> We lack enthusiasm.
> Life seems a mystery;
> It's like the play a lady
> Told me about: "It's not . . .
> It doesn't *have* a plot,"
> She says, "it's history."
>
> (from *A Dream of Governors, 1959*)

What the act and art of poetics demand is a form of intense, naive enthusiasm. By naive, I simply mean that a poetics must be an unexamined intellectual and emotional energy flowing outward; as such, it is opposed to logical analysis and critical thinking: it cannot be balanced. It's a crystallization in essay form of heart truths. But it's a crystallization: it has form and structure, involves vision and revision just as a poem does. In regard to form and structure, it might be interesting to consider the inimical influence of that form which has in the last ten years largely replaced the essay on poetics: the interview. Too often in interviews personality replaces poetry (something our culture would applaud); rather than the pondered testimony of a life lived with and through poetry, we have only the most superficial phenomena: anecdotes, off-the-cuff opinions, and prejudices. The entire quality of the interview is at the mercy of the interaction between interviewer and poet.

In a time when poets seemed content simply to quietly or emphatically write their poems and keep on with business, Robert Bly was determined to think and write seriously about how important poetry is. We see this determination throughout *The Fifties* and *The Sixties* and in an important essay called "A Wrong Turning in American Poetry," which first appeared in *Choice*.

    A good deal has been said about Bly's translations, and it's obvious that his efforts in this field brought about a revitalizing of American poetry. But the same could be said about W. S. Merwin and many others who were actively translating at this time, and yet the impact of other translators was not as strong. Why? Because Bly didn't simply translate, he championed the poets and the ideas about poetry their work embodied. When he translated Rilke, Neruda, Vallejo, García Lorca, Trakl, and (much later) Tranströmer, he did his best to speak about their notions of poetry.

When in conjunction with his translating, Bly affirmed what he called "the image" (and which has since acquired the critical label, "deep image"), he was attempting to reunite American poetry with the mainstream developments of Romantic poetry as it had evolved on the European mainland: a poetry structured by symbolic imagination and making *extensive* (Neruda, surrealism) or *intensive* (Rilke, Tranströmer) use of symbols. If we seek a literary definition of symbol, we might well turn to Pound's definition of the "Image" as "that which presents an intellectual and emotional complex in an instant of time.... It is the presentation of such a 'complex' instantaneously which gives that sense of sudden liberation; that sense of freedom from time limits and space limits; that sense of sudden growth, which we experience in the presence of the greatest works of art" (from "A Retrospect"). Although Pound defined "Image" acutely, his own poetry was not characterized by its use—Pound's was a discursive, didactic imagination, or perhaps a musical imagination, but certainly not a symbolic one.

This notion of image which Bly repopularized is that of the crystallized intelligence of the unconscious mind, and as such it incorporates into poetic theory useful contributions from the dream theories of the depth psychologies of Freud and Jung. What Bly's talk of "the image" accomplished was a naive and necessary affirmation of the symbolic imagination that structures lyric poetry.

If traditional symbolist theory sees the role of the image as the embodied lyric epiphany (either that moment in time that transcends time, or that which fuses and reconciles a poem's opposing forces), then another role for the image is probably at work in the politicized, anarchic intensity of surrealism from which one major aspect of Bly's own poetry is derived. In surrealism, we have a bubbling caldron of images rather than a crystal.

2

Bly's essays, in the historical context of American poetry in the midfifties, represented the most intense public thinking about poetry's human importance that was taking place in English. The response to those essays, then and now, varied greatly: to many young poets, they were inspirational; to many of his peers, provocative; to many of his elders, exasperating and impertinent. Bly kept (and keeps) the pot of American poetics boiling. His pot is a stew: a bewildering richness of ideas and opinions—many of them contradictory, many of them seeming to be only half thought out. His intelligence is usually a moral one, occasionally a moralistic one.

I have mentioned the role of the image and the affirmation of symbolic intelligence as two lasting contributions from the early essays of Bly, but I think any attempt to locate and trace the continuity of his ideas and themes might be wrongheaded. Bly's ideas appear to arrive full-blown from the unconscious and seldom seem the product of discursive thought. In this regard, it might be interesting to quote one of Bly's favorite sources on a form of consciousness he calls the introverted intuitive type:

> The peculiar nature of introverted intuition, if it gains the ascendancy, produces a peculiar type of man: the mystical dreamer and seer on the one hand, the artist and the crank on the other. The artist might be regarded as the normal representative of this type, which tends to confine itself to the perceptive character of intuition. As a rule, the intuitive stops at perception; perception is his main problem, and—in the case of the creative artist—the shaping of his perception. But the crank is content with a visionary idea by which he himself is shaped and determined. Naturally the intensification of intuition often results in an extraordinary aloofness of the individ-

ual from tangible reality; he may even become a complete enigma to his immediate circle. If he is an artist, he reveals strange, far off things in his art, shimmering in all colors, at once portentous and banal, beautiful and grotesque, sublime and whimsical. . . .

Although the intuitive type has little inclination to make a moral problem of perception, since a strengthening of the judging functions is required for this, only a slight differentiation of judgement is sufficient to shift intuitive perception from the purely aesthetic into the moral sphere. (C. G. Jung, *Psychological Types*)

Bly is in large part a teacher-guru of the Way of Poetry—someone to whom ideas about poetry and poetry's role in culture and politics are as important as poems themselves. He has this in common with Gary Snyder, though their styles of presentation differ. If both of them are occasionally obscured by (and resented for) the largeness of their respective followings, we must never forget that their ideas are of utmost importance to poets and people who care about poetry.

Robert Bly has, in his time, changed American poetry: opened up new directions it might move in, inspired some poets to explore these directions, others to react strongly against such prospects. His role, stature, and style seem to me equivalent to that of Ezra Pound in the early decades of this century.

The Two-Way Ladder
Bishop and Lowell

Opposition is true friendship.
—Blake, "Marriage of Heaven and Hell"

In his late poem "The Circus Animals' Desertion," Yeats laments that, old man that he is, he can no longer summon at will those themes that manifested themselves to him as idealized images. He goes on to ponder the relationship between those beloved images and their source in the circumstances of his life and the messy subjectivity of his emotions:

> Those masterful images because complete
> Grew in pure mind but out of what began?
> A mound of refuse or the sweepings of a street,
> Old kettles, old bottles, and a broken can,
> Old iron, old bones, old rags, that raving slut
> Who keeps the till. Now that my ladder's gone,
> I must lie down where all the ladders start,
> In the foul rag-and-bone shop of the heart.

It is interesting and illuminating to consider the thirty-year personal and artistic friendship between Elizabeth Bishop and Robert Lowell in relation to Yeats's architecture of the imaginative life. By temperamental inclination, the two poets resided on different floors of Yeats's duplex. Lowell was at home in the anarchic squalor of the circumstantial and passionate life; Bishop moved comfortably among the icy clarities of masterful images. The secret of the long, fruitful friendship between these two difficult poets is tied to their separate

---

American Poetry Review (1991).

residence but also to their ability to visit each other's abode and gather from it what their art demanded.

Though their friendship was intense from the very outset (Lowell claimed to believe he had proposed to Bishop at their first meeting in 1948), the contrast between their personalities was as pronounced as their respective backgrounds. The shy orphan raised by pious relatives in rural Nova Scotia had only a few important things in common with the sophisticated and pampered only son of Boston brahmins. For one thing, both were serious and ambitious artists whose dedication to their chosen art was central to their lives. The mutual respect they felt for each other's work was a constant, frequently reiterated in the letters that sustained their relationship over the years. They also shared certain powerful afflictions—both had lifelong struggles against alcoholism, both suffered from serious emotional instability. Not least important was that both recognized in the other a survivor—both possessed the stamina and resources to endure their chaotic and painful circumstances and to persevere through them. Despite, or in addition to, their survivor qualities both were haunted by varying degrees of guilt throughout their lives.

Though they were unfailingly nurturing and supportive of each other, those who knew them couldn't help but notice how startlingly different they were personally. Whereas Lowell was extroverted, confident, impulsive, and charismatic, Bishop was shy, even withdrawn in social matters. Bishop avoided the literary world and although she had many friends, Lowell was her only sustained contact with the literati. On the other hand, Lowell thrived on the literary scene, most of his friends being either writers or editors. Bishop was slow in her creative output and rather patient about it, sometimes working ten years on a poem. Lowell, especially after *Life Studies,* was prolific and eager, even impatient, to publish his poems.

Bishop respected privacy and insisted on respect for hers. Even the later Bishop who had turned to the world of teaching and appeared to be more public was still constantly on her guard, as when, in her *Paris Review* interview, she constantly deflected the interviewer's questions with anecdotes. Lowell was a great gossip and a great confessor, even a compulsive one as his life went on. He was driven to turn his life into art, never giving up hope that in the process his "simple autobiography [would] at last become a plot" ("Unwanted," from *Day by Day*). He was also driven to turn other people's lives into art. In the introduction to *Notebook*, he argues that "accident threw up subjects, and the plot swallowed them—famished for human chances." A nice phrase, but in practice this could mean things like taking Bishop's story about her childhood and her mother's final breakdown, "In the Village," and rewriting it as a poem which he prints in 1962 as "The Scream," perhaps forcing Bishop to print it in *Questions of Travel* (1965) as a means of reclaiming it. Or Lowell's notorious use of quotes and rewritten quotes from Elizabeth Hardwick's letters in *The Dolphin*, his sequence about the breakup of their marriage. It was this invasion of privacy that deeply offended Bishop and strained their friendship seriously. Even later, Lowell would make a sonnet from the language of a desperate letter Bishop sent him from Brazil, and apologize for it only after the poem was printed without her knowledge or permission.

The differences in personality and background were inevitably reflected in their literary values and styles. Bishop insists on respecting facts: accuracy and fidelity to the observable world were essential to her art (something her earlier fifteen-year relationship with Marianne Moore had crystallized). In her struggle to resist the existential vertigo of "In the Waiting Room," the young speaker is literally stabilized by facts and dates. To Bishop, fidelity to facts is related to "health," and she enters into serious disagreement with Lowell when his freewheeling translations in *Imitations* seem to her to betray the equally important facts of the original poem's meaning. Lowell, for all the vaunted particularity of his poems, had no such relationship to observed facts, just as he had little knowledge of the natural world. ("My passion for accuracy may strike you as old-maidish—but since we do float on an unknown sea I think we should examine the other floating things that come our way very carefully; who knows what might depend upon it? So I'm enclosing a clipping about raccoons" [David Kalstone, *Becoming a Poet*, p. 213].)

For Bishop, as her image of floating on an unknown sea

indicates, life entailed great jeopardy. If Bishop was consistently oriented by facts, stabilized by her accurate observations of the world around her, we could almost say that facts had a disorienting effect on Lowell, as when the flurry of details in "Memories of West Street and Lepke" only show that the young Lowell, like the "flyweight Abramowitz," is "out of it."

To Lowell, writing *is* life—life isn't real until he transfers it to writing. The writing is what is real: "My sin (mistake?) was publishing (*The Dolphin*). I couldn't bear to have my book (my life) wait inside me like a dead child" (letter of July, 1973, to Bishop). Writing made the life real; he only lived, it seemed to him, to turn his experiences into poems. To Bishop, life and art were separate, distanced. The latter had healing powers not available to the former.

This brief and necessarily superficial sketch of their contrasting personalities and values may be interesting in its own right, but my intention is to explore how the two poets mutually influenced each other's work. My contention is that Lowell persuades (or, more precisely, Lowell's *Life Studies* persuades) Bishop to descend from the high house of Yeats's poem into the risk of dramatizing her self and the issues of her lived life. Reciprocally, Lowell learns from Bishop to make use of "masterful images" to resolve the energies and themes of certain of his best poems, among them "Skunk Hour," "Memories of West Street and Lepke," and "For the Union Dead." Characteristically, Lowell was quick to learn (to appropriate?) from Bishop, but, equally characteristically, the impact was only temporary. Likewise, Bishop, true to her nature, was very slow and even reluctant to learn her deepest lesson from Lowell, but when she did the effect was profound and lasting, and permeated the whole of *Geography III*, her finest book.

In order to understand *why* each needed the other, what each poet had to gain from the other, what the ladder between these two worlds would be worth, it is necessary to characterize the strengths and weakness of both poets' work.

One might say of Lowell without Bishop that his greatest strength was a gift for powerful rhetoric that took the form of what he himself called "phrases that ring for their music and carry some buried suggestion" through "the brute flow of composition" (Anthony Ostroff, *The Contemporary Poet as Artist and Critic,* p. 107). This "mania for phrases" looked to Milton for its harsh consonantal music—"I want words meathooked from the living steer," he says in "The Nihilist as Hero." In addition, Lowell had an eye for particulars (especially as they revealed social, economic, or historical connections) and a sense of intensity and urgency in his presentation of subject matter. His major weakness concerned giving form or closure to his material. Closure is a sign of a poem's ability to arrive at meaning, to cohere. Resolution is, to use Lowell's own words, "if not everything, then the main half of a poem" (Ostroff). Mandelstam says somewhere that the poem asserts a centripetal power against the tendency of things to disperse to the periphery. This essential centripetal power threatens to elude Lowell's poems throughout his career. In the early work he makes extensive use of rhyme and meter for their formal ordering power. But when it comes to resolving the poem, to achieving closure he has trouble bringing forth something from within the poem's material that has resolving power. In *Lord Weary's Castle* (1947), his poems frequently resolve with an image from apocalyptic Catholic mythology, but by the midfifties he has lost that faith. Possibly no other poet has equaled Lowell's power of letting loose in a poem the phenomena of our culture: objects, products, social backgrounds, brand names—the debris proliferates, a density of things in the later poetry as pronounced as the density of rhetoric in his early work. But how to make it cohere in what is essentially a dramatic lyric form? Lowell had great difficulty locating some deeper coherence to offset the powerful disorder his poems unleashed. This was no secret to Lowell—it haunted him amid the splendor of his gifts and rhetoric: "Like thousands, I took just pride and more than just, / struck matches that brought my blood to a boil; / I memorized the tricks to set the river on fire— / somehow never wrote something to go back to." ("Reading Myself," *Selected Poems,* p. 177). He was forever announcing the discovery of the cohering element, as in his late poem "Unwanted" where he again declares that he has found it, that cause that will "give my simple autobiography a plot." But the fact is, he seldom did find that key, that plot or masterful image that could prevent his poems from disintegrating into chaos or becoming (as he says in his last poem) "paralysed by fact."

Bishop without Lowell had the great strengths of observation and description that she cultivated during her fifteen-year relationship with her first mentor, Marianne Moore. She also possessed a gift for thinking in symbols or for using symbolic imagination to tease complex possibilities out of verbal opportunities, as in her famous poem "The Man Moth" where a newspaper misspelling of "mammoth" becomes the occasion for creating a strange character and his story. But her weaknesses, as always linked to her strengths, include detachment and emotional distance from her subjects. "We'd rather have the iceberg than the ship" she says in an early poem, and like her preferred object an early Bishop poem can be nine-tenths below the waterline, invisible and almost inaudible—chilly, unsaid.

In looking first at Bishop's "The Armadillo" and then Lowell's "Skunk Hour," which he claims to have modeled on the former poem, I hope to demonstrate that Bishop gave Lowell the notion that images were a cohering principle capable of ordering the chaos his poems unleashed. Later, I'll look briefly at Bishop's "Crusoe in England," a kind of poem she could never have written without the example and encouragement of Lowell's work.

Although "The Armadillo" did not appear until *Questions of Travel* (1965), it was actually written in the fifties, before any of the poems that would appear in Lowell's *Life Studies* (1957):

The Armadillo
For Robert Lowell

This is the time of year
when almost every night
the frail, illegal fire balloons appear.
Climbing the mountain height,

rising toward a saint
still honored in these parts,
the paper chambers flush and fill with light
that comes and goes, like hearts.

Once up against the sky it's hard
to tell them from the stars—
planets, that is—the tinted ones:
Venus going down, or Mars,

or the pale green one. With a wind,
they flare and falter, wobble and toss;
but if it's still they steer between
the kite sticks of the Southern Cross,

receding, dwindling, solemnly
and steadily forsaking us,
or, in the downdraft from a peak,
suddenly turning dangerous.

Last night another big one fell.
It splattered like an egg of fire
against the cliff behind the house.
The flame ran down. We saw the pair

of owls who nest there flying up
and up, their whirling black-and-white
stained bright pink underneath, until
they shrieked up out of sight.

The ancient owls' nest must have burned.
Hastily, all alone,
a glistening armadillo left the scene,
rose-flecked, head down, tail down,

and then a baby rabbit jumped out,
short-eared, to our surprise.
So soft!—a handful of intangible ash
with fixed, ignited eyes.

Too pretty, dreamlike mimicry!
O falling fire and piercing cry
and panic, and a weak mailed fist
clenched ignorant against the sky!

Beginning as a general narrative description of the phenomenon, the poem in stanza 6 becomes sharply focused in time and place: "Last night another big one fell." The next four stanzas constitute a second, more highly charged drama of the destructive balloon and its four victims: a pair of nest-ing owls, an armadillo, and a baby rabbit. The final stanza, set off from the body of the poem as a kind of coda by its italics, consists of two phrases. The first is an exclamatory comment on the events of the preceding four stanzas. The second phrase involves a transformation and fusion of elements from all the victims: the owls contribute their cry, the rabbit its panic, and the armadillo the metaphor of the weak mailed fist (based on the armadillo's armored bands and its habit of curling up when attacked). The phrase condenses and fuses the whole drama of the balloons gone awry and wreaking destruction on intimacy (the nest behind the house), harming the harmless. There is no need to interpret the last stanza at length; I only wish to emphasize that it brings together threads and images from the whole preceding narrative into a single language unit and a sudden unfolding gesture of falling fire and cry/panic/fist clenched. These final lines liberate the symbolic power latent in the earlier description.

The poem itself was never simply a descriptive narrative. It has in common with a number of Bishop's poems a kind of subliminal plot concerning the relationship between earth and heaven, between a terrestrial world that could be almost paradisal and a supernatural, religious world (a sky world) that acts destructively toward the terrestrial inhabitants, either through moral judgments (the skeletal preacher/lighthouse of "Seascape"), or through violence (the lightning that strikes the church in "Santarém"). In "The Armadillo," a gesture of respect (the fire balloons) goes awry and returns to earth to destroy intimacy and vulnerable innocence. Without wishing to be too biographically analytic, I would point out that the poem's pivot point, where the worshipful gesture turns back, is interesting:

> receding, dwindling, solemnly
> and steadily forsaking us

(the balloons like the gods, like parents abandoning their children)

> or, in the downdraft from a peak,
> suddenly turning dangerous

139

To abandon is one thing, but a worse gesture is possible: for the powerful to turn against and hurt the vulnerable. This drama of a powerful and a vulnerable set of religious or quasi-religious terms recurs throughout Bishop's oeuvre, and she always identifies with the victims.

"Skunk Hour" was the first of the poems in *Life Studies* to be completed, but it was placed last in the collection, another tribute to its enormous powers of resolution:

Skunk Hour
For Elizabeth Bishop

Nautilus Island's hermit
heiress still lives through winters in her Spartan cottage;
her sheep still graze above the sea.
Her son's a bishop. Her farmer
is first selectman in our village;
she's in her dotage.

Thirsting for
the hierarchic privacy
of Queen Victoria's century,
she buys up all
the eyesores facing her shore,
and lets them fall.

The season's ill—
we've lost our summer millionaire,
who seemed to leap from an L. L. Bean
catalogue. His nine-knot yawl
was auctioned off to lobstermen.
A red fox stain covers Blue Hill.

And now our fairy
decorator brightens his shop for fall;
his fishnet's filled with orange cork,
orange, his cobbler's bench and awl;
there is no money in his work,
he'd rather marry.

One dark night,
my Tudor Ford climbed the hill's skull;
I watched for love-cars. Lights turned down,
they lay together, hull to hull,

> where the graveyard shelves on the town. . . .
> My mind's not right.
>
> A car radio bleats,
> "Love, O careless Love. . . ." I hear
> my ill-spirit sob in each blood cell,
> as if my hand were at its throat. . . .
> I myself am hell;
> nobody's here—
>
> only skunks, that search
> in the moonlight for a bite to eat.
> They march on their soles up Main Street:
> white stripes, moonstruck eyes' red fire
> under the chalk-dry and spar spire
> of the Trinitarian Church.
>
> I stand on top
> of our back steps and breathe the rich air—
> a mother skunk with her column of kittens swills the garbage pail.
> She jabs her wedge-head in a cup
> of sour cream, drops her ostrich tail,
> and will not scare.

There have been many excellent line-by-line readings of Lowell's poem by other poets, starting with Wilbur's and Berryman's in Anthony Ostroff's *The Contemporary Poet as Artist and Critic* and extending up to Sandra Gilbert's in a book called *A Book of Rereadings*. They essentially agree about its themes and movement: that this is a dark night of the soul, the spiritual and psychological crisis of an "I" who is surrounded by images of decline and decay (the collapsing houses, the sold-off yacht, the red fox stain). The destruction in the outer world, which we see first, is mirrored in the inner world of the speaker as extreme anguish and disorientation. As Lowell himself says (in Ostroff), "sterility howls through the landscape." "The composition [of early stanzas] drifts, its direction sinks out of sight into the casual, chancy arrangements of nature and decay." All readings agree with Lowell's sense that the poem's themes are brought into focus by the emergence of the skunks in the last two stanzas. To use Lowell's own phrasing, "drifting description" gives way to a "single animal"—a focus.

You could think of "Skunk Hour" as being organized a bit like a whirlpool that slowly spirals toward a center, taking debris with it. The outermost circuits of that funnel are the drifting description of the first four stanzas, then the two stanzas organized around the speaker's own disturbed state of mind and actions, and finally the skunks at the smallest point of the cone. Whether we attend most to the single figure of the mother skunk or to the actions of the final two stanzas, we are clearly in the presence of that complex concentration of meanings that characterizes a symbol.

Lowell calls his skunks (in a letter about the poem) a "healthy, joyful apparition—despite their diet, smell; they are natural power." Without contradicting Lowell, I'd say there is more power than joy in the skunk stanzas: the "march" and the "column," though naturalistically accurate, are also buried military images—the skunks are an occupying army. They are a bit supernatural ("apparitions" with "fire" in their eyes), but also insistently natural: the mother exists in the brute fact of her appetite. She represents an animal life force unrepelled by what might deter the more squeamish; to her "sour" cream is food and nothing will keep her from satisfying her needs. Unlike many of the earlier inhabitants of the poem, especially the speaker, the skunks are purposeful—hunger impels them and focuses their behavior. The skunks convey, above all, the enactment of survival. The agonized speaker "descends" in these final stanzas to the animal level to locate a possible affirmation of his spirit in the simplicities of unconflicted instinctual behavior.

All of this is fairly obvious. We could discover many more possibilities in the skunk image; we could quibble about emphases, but I think most readers would agree about what is going on overall. My point is this: from his admiring and intense reading of Bishop's "The Armadillo" Lowell got his main formal notion for the poem—drifting description that ends in a single animal. This "drifting description" is one form of the recurring crisis of Lowell's work: the self in constant danger of disintegration—inner and outer disorder mirroring each other. How will the self stay unitary and purposeful? How survive? The "courage" and desperation, the animal hunger of the mother skunk give him a symbol in his poem. Unfortunately, Lowell seldom made successful use of symbols in his work: they simply weren't part of his temperament. Though he himself characterized his early work as "symbol-ridden," much of the apocalyptic Catholic imagery he used to resolve those poems feels imposed on the poems' chaos from outside. In a debate with his friend Stanley Kunitz, Lowell referred to symbols as hatracks, and I think that is a wonderfully dismissive image for how he typically experiences them: that you could hang on them any meaning, any hat you arbitrarily chose. But an authentic symbol—Yeats's "masterful image"—is not that at all; it climbs the ladder out of the poem's rag and bone shop with the natural grace and startling presence of the mother skunk swilling the garbage pail.

Nietzsche tells us that the artist must descend into the Dionysiac chaos and lose his or her self entirely in this destructive ecstasy in order to arrive at the Apollonian unitary image that heals—as if you must leap into the sea at night, risk all, so that the moon will rise, beautiful and pure. Lowell leaps, but few symbols (that is what healing images are) reward his risk. At the end of his contribution to the Ostroff book he addresses himself and John Berryman as they both emerge from the latter's fierce reading of "Skunk Hour"—"Thank God, we both come out clinging to spars, enough floating matter to save us, though faithless." In much of his later work, Lowell floats but sees no celestial image to restore or establish his faith.

Though she was repelled by the more egregious of Lowell's appropriations of other people's experience and work, including her own, Bishop was inspired by his risk-taking in bringing himself into the poem. What was pathological in Lowell became humanly deepening in Bishop's later work. For all her fabled reticence, Bishop is far more present in *Geography III* than in any previous collection. Few if any of her earlier poems have an "I" so steadily present and so willing, in understated ways, to assert her anguish as a part of the overall composition in poem after poem. But no poem in the collection permits her such a complete enactment of her story as

"Crusoe in England," a poem so rich and complex we can only touch on certain of its pleasures.

Essentially, "Crusoe in England" is a spiritual autobiography in the guise of a dramatic monologue. It was begun in the midsixties with the working title "Crusoe at Home" and was probably originally intended to be far more celebratory, especially concerning her fifteen-year relationship with the Brazilian woman Lota de Soares. We have Bishop's own testimony that at the outset it had "much more about Friday, but I cut it out." The poem took over ten years to write and was wrenched from its original intent by Lota's suicide in the fall of 1967. Essentially, Bishop had three powerful stabilizing forces in her life: her friendship with Lowell, her relationship with Lota, and her love of Brazil where she and Lota lived together. With the breakup of her relationship with Lota and Lota's subsequent death, she not only lost her most enduring intimate relationship but also the house they had built by a mountain waterfall. With the persona of Crusoe, Bishop is able to confront and dramatize the emotional, geographical, and imaginative landscapes that mattered most to her. Readers of a later generation, beneficiaries of the expansion of subject matter and the frankness that Lowell bequeathed, we are in danger of confusing frankness with emotional risk-taking. Reticence and revelation are always relative to the person, and in the context of Bishop's work this poem's self-revelation is unprecedented.

The themes of the poem, as opposed to the Defoe novel, are the themes of her life. They are the emotional and thematic centers (preoccupations and obsessions) that, thanks to Lowell's example, are brought further into the light of the poem than ever before. The poem's two big risks, its two violations of her previous privacies, concern her homosexuality and, to a lesser degree, her relationship to alcohol ("and so I made home-brew. I'd drink / the awful, fizzy, stinging stuff / that went straight to my head . . ."). Perhaps acknowledging and dramatizing these large and simple privacies permitted her to get closer to other powerful themes: loneliness, her longing for and fear of intimacy, her fears of loss laid down perhaps by all her childhood losses. Heart mysteries here, as Yeats would say; much of the rag and bone shop here.

If the poem's emotional landscape centers on the tensions of solitude and loneliness, the external landscape (always so important to Bishop) is equally revealing. Crusoe's island fuses elements of her beloved Brazilian home (the "cloud dump" echoing her house by the waterfall) with a kind of fictive Galápagos (Darwin's *Voyage of the Beagle* was one of her favorite books, its author one of her heroes of direct observation of nature). Though she borrows only slightly from the Defoe novel, Bishop inherits a central and trenchant quality for her speaker: Crusoe is a survivor and a resourceful one.

Unlike Defoe's materialist hero, Crusoe/Bishop knows that the world, no matter how rich and various it seems, is actually severely limited. Enumerating the natural phenomena of his island, he mentions volcanoes, which one might reasonably expect to be emblems of geological grandeur, awesome in their size and power. Not so here:

> Well, I had fifty-two
> miserable, small volcanoes I could claim
> with a few slithery strides—
> volcanoes dead as ash heaps.

Here observation meets and is subsumed by Bishop's symbol-making power as we see an additional, deeper disappointment lurking in the passage—a number symbolism that profoundly undercuts our sense of the variety and grandeur of the natural world. Fifty-two sounds like a large number, but it has quietly reduced the whole landscape, ironically deflated it: this ("miserable small volcanoes") is *all* you get—the whole pack of cards, all the weeks in the year. *Nothing* is missing and yet what a pitiful whole it is.

Even esthetic joys, where wonder at the world fuses with imagination, are short-lived:

> And I had waterspouts. Oh,
> half a dozen at a time, far out,
> they'd come and go, advancing and retreating,

> their heads in clouds, their feet in moving patches
> of scuffed-up white.
> Glass chimneys, flexible, attenuated,
> sacerdotal beings of glass . . . I watched
> the water spiral up in them like smoke.
> Beautiful, yes, but not much company.

Here the rhapsody of observation and detached imagination so characteristic of her earlier work (such as the Marianne Moorish "The Imaginary Iceberg") is interrupted to assert the primacy of human emotional needs: "Beautiful, yes, but not much company."

When the poem is able to conceive of the contrary of the volcano's limitation and diminishment, it is even more ominous and threatening:

> I'd have
> nightmares of other islands
> stretching away from mine, infinities
> of islands, islands spawning islands,
> like frogs' eggs turning into polliwogs
> of islands, knowing that I had to live
> on each and every one

This nightmare of multiplying islands presents a kind of sterile fecundity, like that of mitotic cell division. Emanating as they do from the island's basic solitariness ("and there was one of it and one of me. / The island had one kind of everything"), these tedious archipelagoes are the products of an Eveless Eden, an uncompanioned solitude.

What rescues Crusoe/Bishop from this desolation and fecundity? "Just when I thought I couldn't stand it / another minute longer, Friday came." It is companionship and human intimacy that were missing and that alone can alter circumstance into meaning. Now even things (objects in the world) can *mean*—they aren't just observed and enumerated now, nor simply used to fend off boredom (like the baby goat), nor elevated into "sacerdotal beings" like the waterspout. Objects take on significance because of their living, human context: "The knife . . . reeked of meaning like a crucifix," she says of an object in her island life. Once that object is removed from its human, sharing, and interacting context it becomes "drained of meaning"—fit only for a museum. When Crusoe/Bishop contemplates the objects he has saved from his island time (umbrella, goatskin trousers, etc.), he says, "How can anyone want such things?" The world of things, no matter how rich and curious, is nothing without the world of values and purpose. Objects in shared, human context become symbols, vehicles for meaning—the knife in this poem, the carved fountain and waterspout in "Under the Window: Ouro Prêto," or, my favorite, the wasp's nest the pharmacist gives the speaker in the late poem "Santarém," a symbol of the healing powers of the esthetic object. Lowell take note—objects become symbols in the living context of a human situation, otherwise they are, as Coleridge says, "fixed and dead."

Throughout the poem, Bishop's symbol-making power takes a subsidiary though important role—the fifty-two volcanoes are not "masterful images" capable of resolving the poem but interim symbols—momentary crystallizations of meaning. The speaking voice, such an important dramatic element in so many of her late poems (the dream of the grandparents' overheard conversation in "The Moose" or the scream in "In the Waiting Room") here becomes the controlling genius of the poem. It is voice that inserts the human, anguished self into the poem. With a deft and various idiomatic voice, she shifts across a whole range of feelings and emotional strategies ranging from sincere direct statement to ironic deflation. It not only creates the personality but has primary responsibility for unfolding the poem's pleasures and affirmations ("—Pretty to watch; he had a pretty body").

If intimacy and companionship mark the advent of meaning in the poem, then without love the world is void and desolate, for, as we learn in these last lines, "Crusoe in England" is above all an elegy. Crusoe's elegy for Friday; Bishop's elegy for her lover who killed herself. Again, it is the speaking voice that brings the heart mystery directly into the final lines; it is voice that resolves the poem with such direct and vulnerable utterance:

>   —And Friday, my dear Friday, died of measles
>   seventeen years ago come March.

Symbols have no role here: "seventeen" means nothing symbolically, nor is it a detail from Defoe's novel, which records no such death—it is just that the speaker, like Crusoe and Darwin, is ever accurate in record-keeping, though the world he inhabits is now a waste place.

In his essay "A General Introduction to My Work," Yeats claims that "all that is personal soon rots; it must be packed in ice or salt." This is a phrase that cuts both ways. Much of Lowell will perish in fulfillment of Yeats's dictum. On the other hand, much of Bishop's early work, packed in the ice of emotional detachment and the salt of ironic distance, lacks urgency, lacks the "reality" and "freshness" she found in Lowell's *Life Studies* (though not, she hastened to add, in the other "confessionals"). Though each was stupendously gifted and ambitious, their most enduring work has, at its heart, the impact of the other's loved and contrary temperament.

IV

Conversations, Comments, and Notes

Conversation at Brockport

The Lost Children

Years ago, as dusk seeped from the blue
spruce in the yard, they ran to hide.
It was easy to find those who crouched
in the shadow of the chicken coop
or stood still among motionless
horses by the water trough.
But I never found the willful
ones who crossed the fence and lay
down in the high grass to stare up
at the pattern of stars
and meandering summer firefly sparks.

Now I stand again by the fence
and pluck one rusted strand of wire,
harp of lost worlds. At the sound
the children rise from hiding
and move toward me:
eidolons, adrift on the night air.

(from *The Red House*)

Stanley K. Rubin: The poem you just read, "The Lost Children," has a terrific sense of loss in it. Would you say something about that?

This conversation with Stanley K. Rubin and William Heyen took place on October 25, 1984, at SUNY College in Brockport, New York. The text is edited from a videotape produced by the Educational Communications Center.

Orr: A great deal of my poetry is based on memory and childhood, and a sense of both loss and the possibility of recovery through the poem. Saying that, I suspect that I'm describing the lyric temperament. It seems to me that lyric poetry tends to locate itself in the intensity of a given moment. Often lyric poets begin writing with an impulse—or maybe it's a continuing impulse throughout their lives—to seek the origins of the self in past moments, and, of course, that would be in childhood, that place where the self is born, where the most significant and therefore the most intense moments have occurred. That has to do with the lyric or, let's say, the dramatic lyric, the lyric where the self is locus and focus of an event.

William Heyen: You speak of "strand of wire, / harp of lost worlds." That theme of the lost children, of now wanting to draw the past together, reminds me of a lot of your earlier work. In fact, I heard just now the word "crouched" which also shows up in *Gathering the Bones Together.*

Orr: There are recurring words for me. I've worked on the poetry of Stanley Kunitz, and he talks about key images as recurring throughout the poet's lifetime. I have discovered key words which recur again and again in my work—"crouched," for example, or "muck," which is a rich word that I love to use. "Kneel" is another.

Heyen: This is a personal question, and if you want to, you can just tell me to shut up. But some people say that one becomes a lyric poet because of a deep and long-lasting hurt, some sort of trauma. When this terrible thing did happen to you, when you were a young man and in an accident killed your brother—do you think you'd be here in this person, as a poet now, if that had not happened?

Orr: I'm afraid to say that I actually do believe the deep hurt theory. I have a continuing argument about that with dear friends whom I respect a great deal; that is, whether poetry comes out of hurt or out of health and exuberance. The more I deal with it, the more I come back to the feeling that lyric poetry at least has a source of hurt, in the wound. What draws us to poetry is that: not the expression of the wound, but a sense ultimately that the wound can be transformed, that poetry is a healing process. That does not mean poetry is therapy. That does not mean that the poet must necessarily be a confessional poet. But the history of personal lyric poetry (starting with Sappho) is the history of obsession, and obsession begins in hurt.

Of course, terrible hurt or terrible events in one's life are not unique to poets. Everyone suffers some hurt or loss, but frequently we look at poets and say that the early deaths of a father and mother were formative events. On the other hand, certainly not everyone who loses a parent early becomes a poet. But I think there is a connection, and I don't think it's a connection that one has to be ashamed of; nor do I think it's one that makes a poet live a fated life of being forever haunted. For example, I don't experience the intensity of being haunted by events that I once did, and yet I don't feel that this threatens my existence as a poet.

Rubin: When did you begin as a poet? What was your earliest consciousness of these matters that you're discussing?

Orr: It would be hard for me to relate the earliest work, let's say the first book, to these particular biographical events. In a sense, they're at the source of the work, but they weren't present in the first book in any overt way.

The first book is a typical lyric poet's first book, melancholic and intense. I did not have the skills of language at that time nor the psychological skills to approach my own life. The first book of poems used as its model what I would call the lucid dream, a dream that is sharply focused and precise but still mysterious. It's certainly not discursive; it's presentational: event follows event, and metamorphosis takes place. Those are the structural elements of that first book.

But part of that world of dream was an evasion of my own personal history and biography; it was a psychological evasion but also an evasion in terms of needing to develop the skill to give form to that experience, to shape it. A poem that has no absolute structure, no sense of wholeness, is a failure.

I knew from the very beginning of writing that I would need to write about my brother's death and my mother's death. Their deaths haunted me, and I hoped poetry might release me. I was haunted by personal guilt and also a sense of the suddenness of loss, a sense that people existed and were then obliterated, overnight—both my brother and my mother died very suddenly. That people could simply cease to exist seemed an unbearable horror that defeated all meaning.

Therefore, you write poems because they assert meaning. They create meanings, or they discover them. I'm a very pessimistic person—I believe poems create, not discover, meaning for the most part. That's an important distinction, but it's not one that I like to dwell on. I'd like to think they discover meanings that are already there in the world, but I fear that the poet's imagination out of its own need creates meaning. Finally, I felt the need to come closer to that personal experience and to try to discover if there was any meaning in it or to create some meaning in it, some meaning that sustains life, which seems to me the purpose of poetry. The forces that work in the poet's consciousness are the mythic forces of Eros and Thanatos, love and death. Even in its encounter with death, the poem has got to discover some meaning, some life force, something to celebrate.

Rubin: By the time of *The Red House,* was there a conscious coming together of these concerns?

Orr: Some of my intentions, in retrospect, were misguided. There's much more of a narrative at work in *The Red House* poems. I have come to the conclusion I'm not a narrative poet. Lyric poets are always haunted by the sense that they can't extend their poems to take in the world—or at least I was.

I wanted also to do justice to a certain historical world that I knew. The "red house" of the title is where I lived with my family in the country from the time I was six to eleven years old. That was a time that I regard as almost idyllic. I was very happy and there were a lot of interesting things there I wanted to celebrate.

The Red House itself is a sequence of about thirteen poems that begins early on and tries to move up through adolescence, through brief narrative lyric poems following this boy figure. But at a certain point it becomes biographical: the brother's death enters and then the mother's not long after. I was trying to go back to that point where I could find the basis for celebration.

One thing I tried to do in *The Red House* and some of the earlier poems in that sequence was to present the ordinary life of an adolescent boy growing up in this rural environment in such a way that what is ordinary is elevated either by the music itself, by language, or by imagination, by discovery of something being more than it is. I was interested in the way light falls through a barn and the vertical slats of a barn, as if the light was like sword blades piercing a magician's box, that transformational imagination or something like that, perhaps, but still to stay in the waking ordinary world, very much opposed to the dream world that my early work first came from. What I learned from that descriptive enterprise is what I could do and what I couldn't do. I find that what I lost was what I value most—intensity. That's a lyric value. That's brought me back away from narrative, from an attempt to be descriptively adequate to the world's variety. I can admire it in others, but it's not my gift.

Rubin: Surely there's lyric intensity in *The Red House*.

Orr: I hope so. If for some reason I was placed against a wall and asked, "What is it in one word that you value most in poetry?" I would say, "Intensity."

Heyen: You know, when Stan and I hear you talk—and you're extremely articulate about these things—we really hear a "mind in the art of finding," as Stevens says. In your essay on Robert Bly you say, "What the art and act of poetics demand is a form of intense, naive enthusiasm. By naive, I simply mean that a poetics must be an unexamined intellectual and emotional energy flowing outward; as such, it is opposed to logical analysis and critical thinking: it cannot be balanced. It's a crystallization in essay form of heart truths." I'm thinking about this in terms of your book on Kunitz, too. How much as a poet do you want to be in control of what it is that you're doing? How much do you want to know about what you're doing? And how much of this kind of thinking is concurrent with the act of the poem itself, or is this an afterview of your books when you're done with them? What about your sense of poetics as you were writing the book on Kunitz?

Orr: It's difficult to say. The constant struggle is to believe that you can become more and more conscious and aware of the processes of your own mind and your own imagination, and yet at the same time, when it comes time to write the poem, all prayers go toward a total silence of your mind and a reception in which you hope you hear a voice inside you saying anything, saying some word whose meaning you don't know, that will begin to form a poem.

In one of the recent poems I read last night, I said, "I hear a blessed humming in my head and I'm its glad amanuensis." That's an accurate description of a certain historical time when I was simply hearing voices a lot and simply listening and writing down, beginning a poem there. I contrast that with the time when I worked on the critical book that was a general introduction to the work of Stanley Kunitz.

Kunitz was my teacher; he's still my teacher and friend, I hope. I learned a great deal from the long three and a half years of studying his work, trying to articulate what is going on in his poems, what they mean and how they work. My original plan was that I could occupy the critical part of my mind with that and continue writing with the other, so that the right hand wouldn't know what the left hand was doing. But it didn't work.

I learned a great deal. It forced me to slow down in my own writing. I learned a great deal about how his poems work and how poems work. As anyone would by writing about another poet, I learned what I believed about poetry. It's inevitable that you project yourself and your own values and perceptions into someone else's work. What you hope is that it's an accurate projection, that it also discovers something authentically there. When the book appears, you can decide whether I'm talking about Kunitz or Orr. I had certain opportunities to see things in his work because of similarities in attitude and experience.

In my own writing while I was working on the Kunitz book, I went even further toward a literary poem with a density of meaning and allusion, which is characteristic of a phase of Stanley Kunitz's work. His work has gone through a lot of changes. But he's certainly one of the most intelligent people I've ever encountered—I mean intuitively intelligent, an associative intelligence, although for Kunitz I think it was the associational intelligence and for Roethke an emotional, gut-level intelligence.

Kunitz's minor at Harvard was philosophy, and that's not ever to be forgotten. His emotional intensity was transferred up into the intellectual and the literary. I think that affected my work as I wrote the critical book; it became more dense, and I began in the middle of the Kunitz book to reconcile myself to the idea that I would write five poems a year. But those five poems would be so compacted and dense with meaning and history and music as to reconcile me to the loss of the pleasure of writing poems. I like to write. It's fun to sit there every morning and write a new poem or work on old ones. The idea of five poems a year struck me as very sad.

When I finished the Kunitz book, it was as though I'd closed a door to a part of my life. Suddenly I began writing poems that were utterly different, much less literary, almost as a kind of reaction against what I see as both a nobility and a dangerous grandiosity inherent in the Romantic tradition.

Rubin: In that vein would you talk about one of your new poems, "After Botticelli's 'Birth of Venus' "?

Orr: One wants all the resonance of history and culture, yet not to be trapped in it. Someone once described a free verse poem as a poem in which over the poet's one shoulder Literature was looking down at the page and over the other shoulder, Speech. These two forces are impinging on that page and the language on it. In the earlier work, while I was working on the Kunitz book, I was paying more and more attention to the advice I was getting over the shoulder from Literature. The poems got so dense and so compacted that my voice literally couldn't lift them up off the page; I couldn't speak them in a voice that approximated anything but somebody reading aloud a poem, and that seemed terribly frightening to me and solemn and dense in a sad way. A lyric poet finally believes in the incantatory magic of language. Also, I wanted to get some of the variety of tone that you get from speech. I wanted things I'd never had in serious poetry: humor, nastiness, vulgarity—all those things that are important human traits.

"After Botticelli's 'Birth of Venus'" is based on the fifteenth-century painting, which probably everyone has seen reproductions of on postcards or in perfume ads. She's the goddess who's born of the ocean and blown on a shell toward shore, where she's being greeted. The tone is flippant, and yet I hope that beautiful and magical painting shines up through the poem, since Venus and Aphrodite, the goddess of love, seems very worthy of being worshipped.

After Botticelli's "Birth of Venus"

Aphrodite, foam-born, blown
shoreward on her wide shell
with the breeze tickling her bottom
and a large crowd gathered
on the beach to greet and gawk.
The authorities there, too—
men with large batons, trained
in mob control.
                          Someone
selling hot dogs and souvenir
brochures of the obvious.
Meanwhile the goddess herself
has that blissed-out, postcoital
expression that indicates
she's not all there—were she a boxer
with a decent manager he'd recognize
that look; right now he'd be

>   tossing in the towel, reaching
>   for a bright silk robe to wrap his pal.
>   (from *We Must Make a Kingdom of It*)

Rubin: There's a very interesting blend of colloquial idiom with mythic reference in the poem.

Orr: I was interested also in the boxing images. There's the manager's signal—you throw in the towel to stop the match. The mythic is that sacred history of time which we hate. Time is death.

Rubin: Time is the opponent for the lyric poet, but he's not against ideas, is he?

Orr: I hope not. The lyric poem expresses the human longing for the unconditional, for the eternal moment outside of time. In its intensity and its anguish, that longing could seem at odds with culture and intelligence, but I don't think it is. I think it's a form of human consciousness.

Heyen: I sure do like Venus's "blissed-out, postcoital / expression."

Orr: A standard theory is that Botticelli was doing these paintings for the Florentine Platonists. Within this intellectual movement sponsored by the Medicis they were translating all of the works of Plato, Aristotle, and also all these strange, mystical texts of Hermes Trismegistus. All this was happening in Florence in this space of about thirty or forty years, and it was an attempt to reconcile pagan mysticism and Christianity and Plato. Which is, of course, absurd. But it was a wonderful, imaginative task. They suspect Botticelli was commissioned to do paintings to express that impulse toward reconciliation. Aphrodite is a pagan goddess, and what you should be painting is the Madonna and Child if you're a reasonable person at that time; but they convinced themselves that Aphrodite was a part of the search for the Good. She was this earthly beauty who was unearthly and would lead us higher toward an ideal beauty. But, of course, she's also a very sexy lady, and in the Botticelli painting you get this odd combination of earthly, fleshly beauty and unearthly beauty—what they call temporal beatitude. That seems to me what all lyric poems want—temporal beatitude.

Rubin: Your poetry has numerous references to art, to literature, to ideas. Yet there's also this concern with the most minute, transient kind of natural life. For you, the two—nature and culture—don't seem to pull apart as sources.

Orr: It seems to me that the struggle in growing is to bring together those different things.

Rubin: Does that have something to do with how you write? Are you in a frame of mind where you'll be very attentive to passing natural life and you'll be thinking about Botticelli or some key work?

Orr: That's an interesting question because it's very much not that way, very much not an awareness of the world in any way such as that, where I see something and write about it. It's never happened that way.

There is a block of time from about eight to noon during which I have written for about fifteen years now as a daily habit. Any other time of the day I do not give a single thought to writing poems or to what I'm working on at all. I don't think about the poems. I don't look for a poem. I don't consider myself a poet. It simply doesn't happen that way.

I have two theories about my composing. One has to do with dreams as models for how disparate things come together and become part of the same story. In dreams things from greatly different times and cultures, along with different people and elements you're not even aware of, suddenly come together in a strange little visual story that you're taking part in. I experience the world, as many people do, as extremely fragmented and fragmenting. In the morning, I'm fresh from dreams, a state of consciousness where things have been made into wholes. Maybe it's not a whole that we understand, but it does form a beginning, a middle, and an end, which seems to me what story is as opposed to narrative—a sense of beginning, middle, and end, all of which are in some kind of meaningful proportion to each other.

The other theory is that all sorts of sensations and phenomena are entering our consciousness in all different ways through all the different senses all day, but as in that old movie about the cosmic rays just passing right through the body, only a few actually hit that strange identifiable shape inside you we call the self and bounce back out. What I use in my poems are not historical or literary references that I've encountered in books but that little word or image that went inside me and came back out again. I'm getting it on the way back out when it's somehow bounced off some part of this thing called the self. Out of the thousands of facts and phenomena a day, most have no real significance to the self, and therefore our connection to them is not the stuff of poetry. But with those few that hit something inside, you try to listen with your ear pointed inward, trying to hear them on the way out again. I have to either see some image or hear some language to start a poem. I've never chosen a subject. Or, when I have, it's been extraordinarily ill-advised.

Rubin: Do you revise much?

Orr: Constantly. Until I went to graduate school, I couldn't revise at all. I'd never been in a workshop, so nobody had really told me what poetry was, but I was writing a lot of what I hoped were poems. In retrospect, they were just struggling to be poems. If something failed or somebody said the poem was not good, I'd write another one. I never felt that I could alter it. It wasn't ego, just ignorance. Revision is extraordinarily profound and painfully difficult for a young poet to learn. At least it was for me. If one of our secret desires is to be loved as we are, then a corollary secret desire is that the poem be perfect as it first appears.

Heyen: I don't know if you'll agree, but I think revision should be no more conscious or rational and no less intuitive than the first writing itself. I like to keep myself in the mind that brought the first flow through, if I can.

Orr: Yes, I think that's true. I now love to revise. I do it constantly, and it seems to me that's where poems happen. If I have twelve poems that I'm working on, the initial products of twelve different days, let's say, than I have an emotional spectrum: this poem began in happiness, this poem began in a melancholy mood, and so on. In the morning I leaf through them and try to work on the one that most corresponds to my mood or my sense of the world that day. The idea that one can wake up happy and work successfully on a morbid poem is absurd. You're not in sympathy with it. For a lyric poem, the need to be in sympathy with a work is the access to the intuitive.

Rubin: Do you have a feeling or conception of audience at this point? Or does that not matter to you in the process of writing?

Orr: It certainly does matter to me, in the process of writing. The narrative of *The Red House* was pushing in a direction that I hadn't sufficient gifts to make interesting or worthwhile to people. The reason for some of the literary density was probably also that secretly and unconsciously I had an audience in mind that saw the lyric poet as semibarbaric. I was trying to prove to someone that culture had not been lost on me. I think a lyric poet fears being accused of being a barbarian or a naive primitivist. I resent that personally. I don't think that a formalist poet is necessarily more intelligent or cultured than a lyric barbarian like myself. I was trying to prove myself to an audience that wasn't appropriate, and I'd gotten too far from myself. I would much rather be intense and risk alienating people. I'm sure that my new work will offend, but that's a good test of art. If it doesn't offend somebody, there's really something wrong.

Some Notes

I've spent a large part of the last three years writing a book about Stanley Kunitz's poetry and I suspect that the book contains numerous of my own opinions about poetry along with a few more objective insights and observations. What follows here is perhaps woefully schematic and abstract, but I'd rather say something than nothing. It might be of some help in terms of orientation to say that the following opinions emanate from a lyrical-mythological perspective on poetry rather than, say, its antitype—a didactic-historical perspective.

We usually live with the Isness of things by projecting onto them the unconscious egotism that structures our day-to-day lives. But when that blank Isness overwhelms the ego (as it does so easily), it seems to me that it calls up something deeper in the human spirit that responds with a deeper affirmation of our existence.

The kind of poem that interests me is one that is called into being as a response to a negation of meaning. The poet's primary task is to discover or create meaning; the poem's task is to embody meaning.

Certainly, personal death is one of the most intense forms of negation, and it calls out of us the meaning-making power— the pattern of magical language that will allow us to live above the abyss without denying that the abyss is there.

From *The Generation of 2000*, edited by William Heyen (Princeton: Ontario Review Press, 1984).

Periodically, our lives intersect with the great mysteries of Eros and Thanatos, or with the lesser mysteries (joy, suffering, rebirth—the list becomes long and personal). These mysteries have the power to move us to that other personal/universal level beyond the ego where something in us creates or discovers meaning.

The poem struggles into being against the negation of the blank page. The blankness of the page is analogous to the blank Isness of things. Such blankness is actually a great darkness. When the words appear they give off light, because each word is a lens that gathers in, intensifies, and focuses what little light there is.

The process of writing happens independently of these ideas. The way poems happen for me has to do with those two most nonrational and ancient forms of meaning: story and symbol, and with the incantatory magic of rhythmical language.

Some Remarks on Craft

A poem should begin strongly. That's a rule of poetry. It should begin with something that really engages us. It seems to me the first half of a poem has to orient its reader, to locate its reader. When you write a poem you're creating a world out of language, and you can be anywhere in space or time. You're creating a whole world and that's one of the things that makes it so exciting to do, but bringing your reader with you creates an enormous burden since your reader needs to know where he is as soon as possible. If he doesn't know, if he's too disoriented, this creates a level of anxiety and he can't pay attention to what's happening.

The observed details, the sensory details—Blake calls them "bright particulars"—make art real, make it important to us. In a poem, it's the difference between saying "the car" and "the blue car." We feel, when we read "the blue car," as if we can see it. Color always works that way. It's a gimmicky particular that makes us feel as though the thing is there. I don't know why it works but it does. It's the sensory details that create out of language something that feels real to us. We take the poem's imagination and set it against our own experience. We want there to be some kind of relationship between the two, and we want the poem to feel real even if it's made up. To create a real, believable world seems to me the ultimate challenge in a poem. And then to make something interesting happen in that world.

From a workshop at Lake County Community College, December 1991.

Every word matters in a poem. In poetry you get an opportunity to deal with two things every time you use a word: one is accuracy and the other is music. In the dream of perfection all poems have, every word is both accurate and musical: accurate and making a contribution to the musical texture of the poem, which is part of its magic. Unfortunately we can't do this all the time, and some people choose one or the other. We all pray the poems we write won't have to make that choice—that they will have compelling music and be totally precise as well.

I have a rule about lyric poems: you don't repeat words unless you do it intentionally for a kind of incantatory effect, as a kind of magical repetition. Incantation is a very primitive and very powerful kind of music. The reason you don't repeat a word in a lyric poem except intentionally is that the reader wants to believe that the imagination of the poet is infinite and that the vocabulary of the poet is infinite, or maybe that the vocabulary is an outward and visible sign that the poet's imagination is infinite. We writers want to believe that too, though we know it's not true, when we write the poem. We know that the first time we draft the poem we repeat words and it's clumsy as hell, but still the reader wants to be constantly surprised, constantly dazzled, constantly seeing something new. When we repeat a word it's a kind of blank, a dead spot; I mean, we've heard it before, so rhythmically it doesn't do anything, doesn't introduce a new event or new sound. We've lost the musical necessity in the poem. To me, even a synonym is better than outright repetition unless that repetition is intentional. A lyric is such a short space that you figure you ought to give your reader his money's worth by as many new sounds and words as possible. But it's probably just a rule meant to be broken.

Out of any given poem a number of successful poems are possible. You could take a poem in this direction and it would become interesting in that way, or you could go in a different direction—you could make it longer and it could become interesting in a certain kind of narrative way, you could make it shorter and it could become more interesting in a lyric way, through concentration, intensification. The way I always work with a poem in a rough draft is by cutting it down to something shorter. That's the thing that temperamentally comes most naturally to me. Aristotle says unity is the main thing in a poem. He says that if we remove some part of a poem and we don't notice that it's missing, then it was never a real part of the whole. That's a wonderful test.

Notebook Excerpts

From 1970 Journal:

Sunday, September 21. 10 A.M.
"Grows smaller"—I love the delicate paradox of that expression. For me, it embodies the absurdity of the static world, the world in which objects are related in an inflexible, proportionate way to each other.

Friday, September 25. Noon.
A dream fragment: unloading a truckful of books at a dock parking area to be loaded aboard a huge ship. One of the books a book of Kandinsky's, illustrated. A girl looking at it, just the captions. I tell her the writing/thought is freaky. In the picture she is looking at there is something about "the hand is a carrot, then it is a rabbit; then you go out in the world and see it is both" or "First the hand is a rabbit, then it is a hand again; then you go out in the world/the daylight and see that it is indeed a rabbit."

Friday, October 2. 10:30 A.M.
My poems sometimes give the illusion of nakedness, but it is a safe nakedness, like undressing in your own room alone. It is not walking naked in a world of people and objects; that would be the true nakedness. My poems are all about the self. My life is all about the self. I can let it in but can't let it out. I can receive, but I can't really give.

These excerpts were selected from daily journals for a 1992 issue of the *Seneca Review* devoted to poets' notebooks and journals.

Naked hour, when suddenly she is no longer there and you can see your mistake: to have thought you could swallow her the way you swallowed the objects of the world and once they had passed through the walls of your body, to set them up in your dark inner kingdom. But you could not swallow her. She was not an object. Now you see the error of your life: trying to swallow everything, unable to let anything out. You see your poems, little maps of the kingdom, showing the new location of the objects you had just swallowed. Now you want to be naked, you want the walls of your body to dissolve into raindrops that fall against the things of this world.

My fear of being swallowed: fear that what I try to do to the world, the world will try to do with me—death, the earth mother.

An old children's "song" I remember from sitting on the back porch in Rensaleerville (age five or younger) and singing it in a slow chant:

> I looked at the moon one night.
> The moon looked at me and went . . .

and then making a farting sound by pressing my mouth against my skin and blowing hard. Singing "moon" with two syllables. Sitting in my father's lap. But it also had something to do, maybe a second verse, with being "gobbled up" and then Dad or someone tickled me and I laughed, but in a scared way. It was at night; there was a moon in the sky. "Gobble you up."

Dreams swallow the objects and people of the world, digest and rearrange them in their kingdom. Just like my poems. My poems are too much like dreams in this way. All take and no give, all swallow and digest; no giving back, no giving to others.

From 1979–80 Journal:

Wednesday, December 19.
Poetry that does not acknowledge or experience the urge to transcend bores me.

Poetry that yields completely to the urge to transcend frightens me, appalls me (and bores me). The watchword of those who wish to give themselves over completely to the ravishment of transcendence is "purity." Beware that term.

Tuesday, February 12.
A lyrical imagination must center itself in the personal, but if the poem goes widely enough we discover that the personal is merely an inner ring of which the societal and historical are more distant, concentric rings. Under the right circumstances, a poem's scope can include a great number of concentric rings.

Monday, February 18.
Historical-lyrical flash: That if you, as a poet, are engaged and sustained by the imagination, you must go to Keats's letters, to Coleridge. If you are responsive to the historical imagination, you should go to Pound's letters.

Pound does not like the Romantics, but more to the point, he does not like or trust imagination. A simple observation to the side: he is a Confucianist—think what position the Chinese Confucianists occupied in relation to their rivals, the Taoists: that tells you where Pound stands.

Perhaps the historical imagination does not like that aspect of imagination which is essential to Keats: the notion of Adam's dream, of imagination itself being creative of truth and beauty. Keats (and Coleridge) give an exalted role to the imagination. Pound does not.

For young poets, Pound is full of good, practical advice. You couldn't get one precise piece of advice about writing from all of Keats's letters. Nevertheless.

Sunday, March 9.
A thought: the failure (of the poem, my poem) is not with the

obsession, but with the limitations of the obsession. It's the same old dilemma of personal and private. My obsessions are inherently personal; I must do all I can not to render them private.

Friday, June 20.
The task of getting back to feeling language inside you, feeling the sounds and rhythms physically. God, that's hard. I feel all this language as being five or ten feet outside me right now—it's getting slowly closer, but it's external; it's like modeling clay or something; it's not inside.

Nor can I transfigure it, or transfigure with it (which is more accurate). Transfigure myself with it.

Monday, June 23.
Some of my best imagining concerns violence, but for every five violence poems I write, only one succeeds in discovering a larger context or meaning. Unless they do discover this larger context, they simply become a discharge of regressive energy. Even that (a regression) can be made meaningful as in "The Gorge" or (perhaps) "Solitary Confinement." But . . . I think I'm inclined to be a little hard on myself about this, too impatient for meanings. Ultimately, things will happen—"The Brave Child," which I like a lot, came after at least five years' preparation.

The role of violence in my psyche is not going to be easily resolved. T. points out that my imagination is most vivid when violent.

So much of this morbid, claustrophobic, sensualized violence in my imagination is centered in that life from twelve to seventeen or eighteen or even later: the horrible sexual desire within and the self-hatred and inhibition all fusing together to form what: a boy who slept with his arms crossed on his chest, his feet crossed, like a sarcophagus lid.

I was "raised" to experience and give my assent to the rural American myth of violence as a boy's blood initiation into manhood/malehood. I see this in the most brute form in James Dickey and Robert Penn Warren. But the hunting accident and Peter's death aborted this whole understanding. I think this later joined with my father's alienation from my mother and her suffering to cause me to fail to link up to the second echo of the myth: man versus woman. A myth demands full participation. I couldn't/can't give that to these myths of male power through violence: I think they represent a compensation for our essential human powerlessness; in the face of nature's indifference and the condition of mortality, we have no real power.

That's what I feel/experience. Back to the old story: the terror of existence. I want to acknowledge that terror (I do/the poems do) and I want to set some things, some stories against it (some poems do that—tell stories that are "momentary stays against terror" rather than confusion).

Right now I have in my daily working to confront a lot of unsuccessful poems about the terror and that can be a little depressing. But I must have faith. And patience.

From St. Paul's "Letter to the Corinthians":
"The Jews seek a sign, and the Greeks seek wisdom."
I'm like the Jews, always seeking a sign, a revelation.

From 1991 Journal:

Friday, May 10.
The horror of Primo Levi's camp stories and the thoughts on the human condition that emerged from his experiences—how I can only take so much of that, then I find myself—as now—reaching for Northrop Frye's essays, which, though occasionally very schematic (as is poetic thought in general, he argues), provide a vision, a transcendent vision that subsumes human suffering to some extent, makes it more bearable. I realize that the mythologies of poetic thought are my "religion"—what makes life bearable to me by integrating personal anguish into a larger scheme—so I can "loose [my]self within a pattern's mastery" (to quote an odd, amazing prose poem of Hart Crane's I encountered yesterday, "Havana Rose").

Thinking about Levi and Frye I think how my favorite Shakespeare play is *The Winter's Tale*—in large part because it begins in the chaos of tragedy and pivots in the middle into the patterns of romance and rebirth and vegetation myth. It goes from a death-world into a birth-world, an Eros world. "It is required you do awake your faith."

As Frankl (in *Man's Search for Meaning*) said about "love" in the death camps: the image of the beloved, "that the poets spoke about," sustained him as nothing else did.

It's a major unitary image behind my "religion"—behind my "religion" of the lyric.

The lyric experience fragments the poet, destabilizes the poet. What restores stability is the possibility of that unitary image, that sustaining symbol.

It needn't always or exclusively be a "beloved" of course, it can also be other things that have become, to borrow Cassirer's borrowed term, "momentary gods."

Someone like Robert Duncan has made a cult of the Beloved, an entire arcane mythology to sustain it and yet, he has that one ravishing lyric that could itself be worth a lifetime's service: "Often I Am Permitted to Return to a Meadow."

Saturday, May 18.
This morning I've flipped over from my "consolidation" mode to my "risk" mode. As I got up this morning I found myself singing the Pointer Sisters' song: "I'm just about to lose control and I think I like it" ("I'm So Excited").

From a Commonplace Book

The Elgin Marbles, brought over by Elgin in two shipments, first displayed in a dingy shed off the Strand—rejected by many experts as being inferior work because they were modeled from nature, but the artists, for the most part, knew. Benjamin Haydon, on his first visit, sees the radius and ulna pressing against the skin in Apollo's wrist.

The marbles didn't correspond to the dominant concept of idealization—the neoclassical mode—where neither bone nor muscle show. Ennobled, boneless.

My own work—when it's too far from reality, from dramatic situation in the world, it becomes "music"—it becomes "boneless." Even the lyric must be grounded; especially, the lyric must be grounded in the world.

Keats's longing for, joy in his loss of self. What he celebrates in *Endymion* as:

> Richer entanglements, enthralments far
> More self-destroying

My favorite poems are Keats's "Lines Supposed to Have Been Addressed to Fanny Brawne" and "Ode to a Nightingale." In the latter, a desperate escape from the self; the parabola of ecstasy the poem describes. In the former, the desperate need for intimacy and the manipulations the speaker orchestrates to try to accomplish the satisfaction of his anguished longing. Seeing myself in both "rich entanglements."

"My self, my Sepulchre, a moving grave . . ."
                                    Milton, *Samson Agonistes*

The moral imperative of history is: Remember! It connects us to the past through memory.

The moral imperative of poetry (art) is: Transform! It connects us to the future through imagination and the past through memory as imagination.

"To restore continuity between the refined and intensified forms of experience that are works of art and the everyday events, doing, and sufferings that are universally recognized to constitute experience. Mountain peaks do not float unsupported; they do not even just rest upon the earth. They *are* the earth in one of its manifest operations."

Dewey, *Art and Experience*

Thinking yesterday how the internal, psychic drama that animates a personal lyric has been there since Sappho first used (created) the word "bittersweet" (*glukupikron*) to describe love. The word stands for the battle of contraries and, to some extent, their linguistic reconciliation.

The sensuous and the mellifluous are not identical in poetry; the sensuous clots and startles, clots and startles as in Keats; not Tennyson.

Vowels and consonants: Mandelstam proposes a split heritage for the Russian language—vowels and words dominated by vowels are a consequence of the priestly invasion—the Greek Gospels brought in and imposed; consonants come from secular Russian, guttural earth and soil. "Russian verse is saturated with consonants and clatters and clicks and whistles with them. Real secular speech. Monkish speech is a litany of vowels." Mandelstam endorses the consonants, the peasant source. Seamus Heaney proposes a similar myth/mysticism of sounds for himself: the harsh consonants of the British invaders and occupiers; the lush vowels of native Irish names and words. He overlays this scheme with harsh, male Protestant and nurturing, female Catholic as well.

Roethke—the genius of dramatic structure: the "Lost Son" sequence is modeled on the central experience of Roethke's

175

psychic life—his episodes of manic-depression. In writing the poem, he reverses the sequence of the mania and the depression so that "we end in joy."

By reversing them, he creates a redeeming order—a drama of redemption, of descent into disorder and then an ascent to the order of meaning/emotion/exultation.

He wrestles his demon, extracts a spiritual blessing, a moral structure from his affliction.

What we call a poet's vision is his or her transformation of obsessions into a spiritual principle or principles. This is the mainspring of lyric vision. Nothing more, nothing less.

Beneath every line of a lyric poem, a voice is whispering "we are mortal."

"Language is the light of the emotions."
    Paul Ricoeur, *The Symbolism of Evil*

Memory is a province, a very large province, in the realm of imagination:

Phil Levine writing a poem about the 1941 race riots in Detroit, decides to look in *Life* magazine to bolster his memory. Says, wait a minute: the streetcars on Woodward Avenue didn't look anything like that; the people didn't dress like that. Memory is imagination. Everything is transformed by memory.

Memory (mother of the Muses) was known as "the waker of longing" according to Gilbert Murray; "the enchantress who turns the common to the heavenly and fills men's eyes with tears because the things that are now past were so beautiful."

Where memory is imagination, an idealizing. Where memory is elegy.

A recurring feeling of late that I don't like Stevens's work because of its recipe of proportions: there is too little world and too much imagination; too little world and too much rhetoric. His work seems to me to be a lemon meringue pie with not enough lemon filling, too much meringue.

"La vie fourmille des monstres innocents" ("Life swarms with innocent monsters"). From Baudelaire's "Mademoiselle Bistouri" ("Miss Scalpel" from *Paris Spleen*)—one of the greatest prose poems. For once, in that verb "fourmille" (derived from "ants"), French is concrete, connected to the world.

Experimentalism and literary avant-garde tied to the "dehumanization" of the plastic arts as they go abstract; to Kandinsky's vow to remove "story-telling" from painting. In painting, the rise of formalist esthetics. In poetry, an abandoning of content, of subject matter. What I resist.

In Hart Crane's poetry, the disordering energy always tended to overpower the "pattern" he conceived to contain it. Even the act of making poetry was more disordering than ordering and involved the destruction of the making self: "The bells, I say, the bells break down their tower." Against Crane's line (as a Yeatsean counter-truth) I'd place Roethke's equally poignant articulation of poetry-making as, in the aggregate, stabilizing for the poet: "This shaking keeps me steady. I should know."

Prose can tell us *How* we live, but only poetry can tell us *Why* we live.

All meanings have pattern, but not all patterns have meaning.

"Some few men have the capacity to confuse their own drama with that of humanity—and this is their salvation." (Sartre on Mallarmé, but it could be said of most poets.)

"But genius is nothing more nor less than childhood recovered at will."
      Baudelaire, "The Painter of Modern Life"

177

How Bishop's biblical references are a form of (symbolic) meaning in her work as when her parody of Noah's "two of everything" in "Crusoe in England" is an index of her desolation and isolation, how cut off she is from love and intimacy:

> "The island had one of everything."

A line that mocks the world's variety with an underlying monotone: forlornness.

Vasko Popa saying to me: you American poets need to learn to say "we" in your poems instead of "I" all the time. Said as a well-intentioned rebuke. Sadly, it really seemed a giant compensatory fantasy on Popa's part—a means of coping with the horrible self-divisions and hatreds that are "Yugoslavia's" historical reality (both past and present). Americans don't do it that way: our great poem, "Song of Myself" doesn't (so far as I know) use the pronoun "we" more than a few times (and then only when "I" and "you" have joined in intimacy). Whitman's assertion: "what I assume you shall assume"—an invitation to sympathetic identification with an other, one self to another self, that's how it's done.

Whitman notebook entry: "Be simple and clear—Be not occult."

UNDER DISCUSSION
Donald Hall, General Editor

Volumes in the Under Discussion series collect reviews and essays about individual poets. The series is concerned with contemporary American and English poets about whom the consensus has not yet been formed and the final vote has not been taken. Titles in the series include:

Elizabeth Bishop and Her Art
edited by Lloyd Schwartz and Sybil P. Estess
Richard Wilbur's Creation
edited and with an Introduction by Wendy Salinger
Reading Adrienne Rich
edited by Jane Roberta Cooper
On the Poetry of Allen Ginsberg
edited by Lewis Hyde
Robert Bly: When Sleepers Awake
edited by Joyce Peseroff
Robert Creeley's Life and Work
edited by John Wilson
On the Poetry of Galway Kinnell
edited by Howard Nelson
On Louis Simpson
edited by Hank Lazer
Anne Sexton
edited by Steven E. Colburn
James Wright
edited by Peter Stitt and Frank Graziano
Frank O'Hara
edited by Jim Elledge
On the Poetry of Philip Levine
edited by Christopher Buckley
The Poetry of W. D. Snodgrass
edited by Stephen Haven
Denise Levertov
edited by Albert Gelpi

Forthcoming volumes will examine the work of William Stafford and Gwendolyn Brooks, among others.

Please write for further information on available editions and current prices.

Ann Arbor   The University of Michigan Press